THE GALLAGHERS *In Their Own Words*

Harry Shaw

Oasis
"Talking"

OMNIBUS PRESS

OASIS *Talking*

Cover & Book designed by Fresh Lemon.
Picture research by Nikki Lloyd & Sarah Bacon.

ISBN: 1.84609.160.8
ISBN13: 978-1-84609-160-5
Order No: OP51282

Exclusive Distributors
Music Sales Limited, 8/9 Frith Street, London W1D 3JB, UK.

Music Sales Corporation,
257 Park Avenue South, New York, NY 10010, USA.

Macmillan Distribution Services,
53 Park West Drive, Derrimut, Vic 3030, Australia.

To the Music Trade only:
Music Sales Limited,
8/9 Frith Street, London W1D 3JB, UK.

Photo credits:
Front cover: Chris Floyd/Camera Press, back cover: LFI

All other pictures supplied by: Dave Fisher/Rex Features, LFI,
Angela Lubrano, Rex Features and Richard Young/Rex Features.

Every effort has been made to trace the copyright holders
of the photographs in this book but one or two were unreachable.
We would be grateful if the photographers concerned would contact us.

Printed by Caligraving Ltd, Thetford, Norfolk.

A catalogue record for this book is available from the British Library.

Visit Omnibus Press on the web at www.omnibuspress.com

Introduction 6

Round Our Way... Manchester 8

Problem Child... Noel Owns Up 11

Hello... The Early Years 13

Married With Children 19

Sex

Fatherhood

Changing Partners

Larging It 32

Drugs

Drink

Rock'n'Roll Star... The Music 39

Wibbling Rivalry... Noel & **Liam** 43

The Famous Five... Noel & **Liam On Oasis** 52

Champagne Supernovas... Wealth & **Fame** 55

The Masterplan... Heroes & **Influences** 63

Stone Roses

Punk

Miscellaneous

Beatlemania

Paul Weller

On Other Groups

Noel & **Liam** v **Pete Doherty** 80

Look Back In Anger – Oasis v **Blur** 82

Rock The Vote... Oasis Play Politics 86

Cast No Shadow... Songwriting 90

The Records 98

Behind The Image 116

Taking On The Tabloids 119

Brothers In Arms... The Fans 121

Up In The Sky... Ambition, Success & **Arrogance** 124

Stepping Out... Oasis On Stage 129

Festival Fever

Oasis On Tour

The States & Americans

Over The Top – Violent Tendencies 141

Oasis Outs & **Ins** 147

Brits, Brats & **Ivors – Awards** 155

Over the Horizon... The Future & **New Beginnings** 158

Barcelona Barney

Rest... In Peace?

CONTENTS

❝ It proves we've done everything we said we would, and it's as much a success for our fans as it is for us. There are ten bands in the Top Ten, five in the Top Five, but there's only one at Number 1! ❞

The words are those of Oasis guitarist and songwriter Noel Gallagher after 'Some Might Say', their sixth single, reached the top in May 1995. By knocking teen idols and fellow Mancunians Take That (including Robbie Williams) off the top, they struck a blow for music – but the message was clearly to Londoners Blur, Oasis's bitter rivals in the 'Battle of Brit-Pop' that occupied the charts and the headlines for most of that year.

Introduction

For a few short publicity-fuelled months, the two groups' rivalry was something akin to The Beatles and the Stones in the Sixties. And though Oasis's musical inspiration came squarely from The Beatles, the Gallagher brothers – outspoken vocalist Liam was the other – were clearly more than comfortable to inherit Jagger and Richards' mantle as kings of controversy. The war of words with Blur is now ancient history, but the brothers have gone on to attack other groups and artists, former members of Oasis and, most colourfully, each other. An interview disc, the intriguingly titled *Wibbling Rivalry*, contained enough personal invective to curdle milk, while Liam's non-appearance on screen for a Jools Holland-hosted TV show led to the terse comment from Noel: "He's lost his voice... and his job."

The senior sibling evidently relented – but such a volatile combination of talents would clearly take some management. And so it proved: tours of the States (1996) and Europe (2000) were interrupted by the departure of Noel, seemingly unable to stomach the behaviour of his

 brother. At least after the Gallaghers' Barcelona barney the band continued with a substitute guitarist in tow, for which an unusually contrite Noel later confessed himself grateful.

The departure of long-time guitarist and bassist Paul 'Bonehead' Arthurs and Paul 'Guigsy' McGuigan in 1999, combined with the formation of own label Big Brother (after the collapse of Creation) seemed likely to intensify Noel's control of the band. But, as their first studio album of the new millennium (and their fifth in total), approached, it seemed other members – and even Liam – might be allowed to break the elder Gallagher's hitherto vice-like creative stranglehold. Perhaps parenthood had mellowed the man... even if both his marriage (to blonde 'rock chick' socialite Meg Mathews) and Liam's (to blonde 'rock chick' singer/actress Patsy Kensit) had ended in very public disarray.

Though they'd released nothing save a patchy live album for some years, the brothers Gallagher were newsworthy enough to bag a front cover of *New Musical Express* in the autumn of 2001, simply for being themselves. And, sure enough, their pronouncements about the state of music, the state of the world (including the then-fresh Afghan conflict) and the state of their complex lives made headlines across the entire media spectrum in the days that followed.

The lesson was clear – write off Liam and Noel at your peril. Because when it came to confounding the critics and winding up Wapping (and the rest of what was once Fleet Street), the Gallaghers still have few equals.

But their first studio album of the new millennium revealed that other band members – even Liam – were being allowed to break the elder Gallagher's hitherto vice-like creative stranglehold. Perhaps parenthood had mellowed the man – even if both his marriage (to blonde 'rock chick' socialite Meg Mathews) and Liam's (to blonde 'rock chick' singer/actress Patsy Kensit) had ended in very public disarray. Though they'd released nothing save a patchy live album for some years, the brothers Gallagher were newsworthy enough to bag a front cover of *New Musical Express* in the autumn of 2001, simply for being themselves. And while their progress through the 'noughties' was far from as naughty as previous form would indicate, the UK chart-topping performance of 2005's *Don't Believe The Truth* and its first single 'Lyla' proved that there was still room for them in the world's record collections. And there's no danger they'll shut up completely – which is good news for the tabloids, because if Oasis didn't exist they'd have to invent them. In Liam's sage words, "We have to give you lot something to write about or you'd be stuck with Travis and Coldplay." Anyone arguin'?

INTRODUCTION

Round Our Way...
Manchester

❝That Manchester scene, right, it took those bands ages to get into the charts. And that was with a scene – loads of idiots walking about in flares. We've just popped up now, and the first single's gone in the charts. Don't need a scene, man. Know what I mean?❞

LIAM (1994)

❝When you play Manchester, you've got this audience and you're never sure how they feel about you. They seemed all right, but they could have been shit. I knew there'd be people there slagging us off for moving out of Manchester and having a Cockney drummer, or whatever. There's a lot of bitterness.❞

LIAM (1995)

❝I'm sure there are loads of people in Manchester who hate us doing well. And there's loads who suddenly want to be best mates. I mean, I was banned from the Dry Bar, but the other day they tried to get me to sign some picture for them like nothing had happened. I don't need those people. It's their problem if they can't handle us being successful.❞

LIAM (1995)

"As soon as I got some money, I was out of there. In Manchester I was sick and tired of going into pubs I'd been going into since I was 15 and everyone saying, 'Tight bastard!' if I didn't buy drinks and 'Flash Bastard!' if I did. I was sick and tired of young crackheads coming up to me in clubs sticking a screwdriver in me back and saying, 'We're doing the merchandising on your next tour' or 'We're going to be your security team.'" NOEL (1996)

"When we began to be successful, we realised that it's really a little hole. That's why I've moved to London; Manchester is too frustrating for me now. When I was young, it was frustrating enough because there was no work and only three usable pubs, but I amused myself there. I go back there at weekends, that's enough for me at present. Of course I'll have to go back there to live one day." NOEL (1996)

"At the end of each road was the factory, and when it finished by closing, all the houses began to empty. In the north of Manchester there are whole streets of empty houses and, saddest of all, in there are the homeless." NOEL (1996)

"Liam... hasn't done a stroke of work for three months. I can't bear lazy people who sit around all day and pontificate on how great they are but don't go and put it on wax man. It reminds me of a lot of people in Manchester. It's like 'I'm this and I'm that', well all right let me hear it, play it me through the speakers and I'll be the judge of how great you are and it's like, 'You ain't got nothin' to play me, so why don't you shut the fuck up?', which is my theory on it all." NOEL (2001)

"I never look forward to (playing) Manchester 'cos there's too many people trying to get on the guest list. The hour-and-a-half on stage will be mega, but the bit before and the bit after will just be a pain in the arse, 'cos it will just be people who think you recognise them but you're not too sure if you do, it's like 'Eh, remember me, I was in your class in St Mark's?' And I'm like 'Really?'" NOEL (2001)

MANCHESTER

"In the early days they used to say we were a Manchester band and we were like 'Well, what the fuck does that mean?' We don't sound anything like the Roses or the Mondays or James, I don't think we sound like any band that came out of Manchester. We're closer to The Buzzcocks than anyone else. The problem is when you say Manchester band you just get this vision of fucking maracas and baggy flares.**"** NOEL (2001)

"We were never sick of Manchester. I mean it was where I was fuckin' born man, how can you get sick of the place where you're born? You couldn't. I think it's a shame that we had to leave there... but you make your decisions in life and you stick by them." NOEL (2001)

"If I didn't have kids I'd be on the train like a shot let me tell you, 'cos I've just about had it with London. It gets on my tits.**"**

NOEL (2001)

Problem Child...
Noel Owns Up

❝It all started because I was a bit of a rogue when I was young.
I used to wag school and be into fuckin' glue-sniffing and stuff.
Then me and this lad robbed our corner shop, which is a very
stupid thing to do 'cos everyone knows exactly who you are.
Anyway, I was put on probation and I got grounded for six months.
I had absolutely nothing to do.

❝Everyone else was going out and I couldn't be bothered doing my
fuckin' homework. So I just sat there playing one string on this
acoustic guitar. I thought I was really good for about a year until
someone tuned it up. Then I thought: 'I can't play the fuckin' thing
at all now. I'm gonna have to start all over again'.❞ NOEL (1994)

❝On the one hand, our mam's
really proud of us. She wants to
show all the neighbours when
we're in the paper. Then she
reads it and she's embarrassed.
I mean, you can act hard when
you're in a band but as soon as
we go home, she sits us down
at the kitchen table. She tells
us we swear too much and
says: 'So what's this about you
sprinkling cocaine on your
cornflakes, Noel? And Liam,
is this true about you going to
whorehouses?' There's
nothing we can say.❞

NOEL (1994)

NOEL WITH HIS MUM

OASIS *Talking*

“I'm a loner, always have been. For the first few months of Oasis, being around loads of people was great 'cos it was something different for me. It's really doing my head in now, though. I get on with the rest of the band all right but the difference is, I was a roadie for five years before Oasis. I've been to America, Argentina, Russia, Japan, all over the world.

“There's nothing that's new to me in the music business any more. I've met the record company executives and the bullshit producers and I know that they're all arseholes. I've already done all that groupie shit that the rest of them do now and believe you me, I had a fuckin' great time. I was as loud as our kid is. I did the same things he does every night.” **NOEL (1994)**

“**Anything over six letters and that's me gone. Sometimes I give lyrics to Liam and two key words of a sentence will be missing. When I gave him, 'Don't Look Back In Anger' he sang something completely different. When I told him he said, 'Well that's not what's written here, chief.'**” NOEL (1996)

LIAM WITH THEIR MUM

“I remember my mum sitting me down one night and saying, 'What is going to become of you?' and I didn't have an answer. But she never once told me to get a proper job or settle down and get married. She just used to say, 'You'd better not let me down,' and I've not.”
NOEL (1996)

Hello...
The Early Years

66 (Creation Records boss) Alan McGee just happened to be at a gig we done in Glasgow, for some bizarre fucking reason. We came on and, midway through our second song, he jumped on stage, came straight up to us and went, 'Have youse got a record deal, man?' And we went,'No'. And he went, 'D'youse want one?' 99 NOEL (1994)

66 **We thought he was taking the piss, 'cos he was all Armani'd up, a bit of a smoothie, like. And he said to me, right, to this day, he doesn't even know what the fuck he signed the band for. Something got him in there, he got butterflies in his stomach, and he just went...** 99 LIAM (1994)

66 What it was, right, I weren't into music. I'd be like, shut up with that bunch of crap you're playing on the guitar, you can't play it, shut up. I was into football, and being a little scally and that. 99 LIAM (1994)

NOEL WITH ALAN McGEE

66 **The worst thing was knowing that I was miles better than the Inspirals – miles better. But I needed the money and I stuck it out 'cos getting a band off the ground is difficult.** 99

NOEL, ON STICKING WITH INSPIRAL CARPETS AS ROADIE (1994)

OASIS Talking

❝The last time I saw him (his Dad) was when two paramedics were carrying him out of the house to hospital. I beat him up. I was sick of all the years of physical and mental abuse he put me through.❞ NOEL (1995)

❝**I remember my first experience of being cool: when I was in primary school I had a kidney infection for years, so I was the only kid allowed to wear long trousers. The others had these little grey shorts like something out of *Kes* and I had these dead cool black skin-tight trousers with little Doc Martens – everybody hated me.**❞ NOEL (1996)

❝I wrote my first song in my bedroom. Winter time. It went G, E minor, C, D, the basic chords, right, and the chorus was, 'And life goes on, but the world will never change.' I must have been smoking too much pot at the time. It was, I dunno, just to see if I could do it. After that I wrote about 75 songs no one's ever heard.
❝The second stage for me was when I was about 20. I started playing at parties and they'd go, 'Wow. You should be a professional.' That got me over the hurdles of playing my songs to other people – nobody actually laughed at me. After that I was out to conquer the world, man.❞ NOEL (1996)

❝**We all started off working for Dad, but the worst thing in the world is working with your dad. You can't do anything right. People ask what it's like being in a band with your brother and I think, 'What about being on a building site in January when it's hailstoning with your Dad and your two brothers and two of your cousins and two of your uncles and you fucking hate the lot of them?'**
❝**I quit and got a job with a building firm who sub-contracted to British Gas. And the pivotal moment of my entire life was this: a big steel cap off an enormous gas pipe we were laying fell on my right foot and smashed it to bits. When I came back from the sick, they gave me a cushy job in stores handing out bolts and wellies. Nobody would turn up for days on end. After about six weeks I started bringing me guitars in and I wrote four of the songs from the first album in that storeroom.**❞ NOEL (1996)

66 Being with Inspiral Carpets was a great chance to suss it all out for three or four years. Being around managers, agents, record company people, journalists. I'd just sit there never saying a word to anyone. NOEL (1996)

66 One of the greatest lyrics that Morrissey ever wrote – and he's a Gemini, same as me – the one that stuck in my head for years is 'You should not go to them. Let them come to you'. I always knew that's how it was going to be. And lo and behold, the chancer that I am, it fucking happened. I couldn't believe it when Alan McGee walked up to me in that club and said, 'Do you want a record deal?' I had to turn away and smirk to meself. To be quite honest, we'd have signed for anyone. But it was only Creation Records – Jesus & Mary Chain, Primal Scream, My Bloody Valentine. Give us it! I believe in fate and I believe it was all mapped out. 99

NOEL (1996)

THE EARLY YEARS

❝Listen, that first gig, there was 40 people maximum there and we had a song called 'Rock'n'Roll Star'. People were going... 'Yeah, course you are mate, bottom of the bill at the Boardwalk on a fuckin' Tuesday night.' Pretentious arseholes is what they thought we were. Went down like a fucking knackered lift. We thought they were going to be in raptures. And it ended in this bowl of silence. But from that first gig on, I don't know what come over us. We knew we were the greatest band in the world. We'd go, 'Fucking Happy Mondays, Stone Roses, they haven't got the tunes we've got'.❞ NOEL (1996)

❝My dad was a DJ so maybe I inherited my musical instincts off him. That's about the only thing he ever did for our family. From my mum, I inherited honesty and hard work. All the good things come from my mum, all the bad things from my dad.❞ NOEL (1997)

❝Me dad had a bad ass and so have I!❞ LIAM (1997)

"Didn't really enjoy school much. Didn't enjoy growing up. Didn't enjoy anything until I was maybe 18. We never had any jobs. We were all unemployed and shit like that. I just remember spending hours and hours sat alone in my room playing guitar, quite isolated and cut off from everyone." NOEL (1997)

"Rain? They were rubbish! Terrible! Absolutely dreadful! Then they changed their name to Oasis and then I went to see them again and they were just as bad. But they had a different singer which was our kid. And he asked us to join the group. I had fuck all better to do, so I said, yeah, I would." NOEL (1997)

BONEHEAD

"I'm not nostalgic about being skint, and being in a fucking van with Liam while he's pissed and Bonehead while he's pissed and me steering. They were good days... The Water Rats and stuff like that was good." NOEL (1997)

"The best bit about them early days was when our kid got chinned. That geezer jumped on stage and lamped him in the eye...."
LIAM (1997)

"Liam might sit here and might make smart quips about (the early days) all afternoon, but he fucking knows what it was like. It was like the Magnificent Seven riding into town, and for an hour they were getting it." NOEL (1997)

"There were seven of us. There was Jason and Coyley as well, and we were having it. Fucking big, large one. Every night. I saw him in

THE EARLY YEARS

a room, right, with a fire extinguisher in one hand and a chainsaw singing (choirboy falsetto) 'You and I are gonna live forever...' (Chainsaw noise) Rrrrrreeeeeeeaargh!' **99**

NOEL (1997)

66 We were crazy. We should have died. But I don't believe in death. Death is just a thing, whatever it is. 99

LIAM (1997)

66 I was actually known in roadie circles for not getting my hands dirty. The Inspirals played a lot of universities, which meant there were always Student Union-types willing to lug speaker cabinets up five flights of stairs! 'Come on Jeremy, get that up there!' Actually, a funny story. I bumped into Tom Inspiral for the first time in five years at a Liverpool Dockers' benefit. I hadn't seen him since the day he sacked me and he came out with the immortal line, 'So what have you been up to?' I just laughed at him and said, 'Y'know, this and that'. **99**

NOEL (2001)

INSPIRAL CARPETS

66 I think he (his dad) resented the fact he had kids because we got in the way of his lifestyle. And we got hammered for it. 99 NOEL (2001)

Married With Children

Sex

❝I'm in this job for the music. It's the most important thing in my life and I'd choose music over any relationship. I can't hold down a relationship with a girl for longer than six months.**❞** NOEL (1994)

❝When we started there were loads and loads of groupies. But it calmed down a bit 'cos everyone has a girlfriend so there is no real need for it. The girlfriends don't come on tour though, stuff that. It's just a laugh, young boys being out on the road together. You've got to keep a certain frame of mind to play in front of 10,000 people.❞ NOEL (1996)

❝Birds are all right. They're all pink on the inside. Any bird who's fit is all right, unless she's nicked or ugly and she speaks backwards to you. If she thinks I'm boss, then thumbs up. Chicks in Japan don't even ask your name, just 'Can I sleep with you tonight?' Certainly, my dear. I like American birds till they open their mouths. Then they annoy me. But if they're fit, they're fit.**❞**

LIAM (1996)

OASIS *Talking*

"It's (marriage) not mellowed me, it's just made me feel more important. 'Cos someone wants to spend the rest of her life with me - it's nice." LIAM (1997)

"That was bollocks. We were meant to be getting married and all the press started getting silly so we fucked it off. But all those different places: I don't know where all that came from. We were going to go to the place where all the champagne and flowers were, but fucking everyone knew about it and I've got eight grand's worth of bleeding champagne in my house. Fucking loads of it, coming out of my ears. Sick of it.**"** **LIAM (1997)**

"It finally happened at Marylebone Registry Office, half seven in the morning, in my jeans. It was top. Me, Pats, the builder whose doing my house and her hairdresser. Just kept it really small, otherwise we were never going to get it done. And we thought, if we go on honeymoon everyone's going to follow us, so there's no point. We reckoned we'd leave it for a bit. That was it: just stayed in a hotel for three days and got off it. Like you do." LIAM (1997)

"We're both moody bastards (Liam and Patsy). Both singers, man, aren't we? She was top. I bought that 'I'm Not Scared' when it came out. Top. Sexy as fuck.**"** **LIAM (1997)**

"In the old days Liam was difficult and drinking so heavily because of his ex-wife (Patsy Kensit). She made him unhappy and he used to take it out on the rest of the band." NOEL (2001)

"If you think I'm over the moon to be here, you must be tripping. Patsy's gone and taken the furniture with the solicitors. I don't even have a tea-bag to my name.**" LIAM ON STAGE (2000)**

"We're going to be together (with Meg) for ever – and if that's not rock'n'roll, too bad." NOEL (2000)

LIAM WITH EX-WIFE PATSY KENSIT

❝Throughout our time together I never cheated on Meg. I left because I could no longer tolerate her behaviour.❞

NOEL (2001)

❝When one person gets married their wife talks to your girlfriend and she says, 'If she's getting married, I want to get married too.' And before you all know it, you're all fookin' married. It's all a con.❞ NOEL (1997)

❝I don't talk about (marriage to Meg) because people don't appreciate my honesty on the subject. There's too much fucking fall-out and I can't be arsed.❞ **NOEL (2001)**

❝What I went through wasn't painful. It was a release for me. It was like, well, thank the lord that's over. I wouldn't bore you with the subject. It's in the past. It's gone.❞ NOEL (2001)

❝For about a year leading up to Meg getting pregnant I was thinking 'This ain't gonna work'. Then Meg got pregnant and it was okay because they're nice and mellow when they're like that. After that it went pear-shaped, getting back to the way it was, the constant larging it. I just couldn't be doing with it any more.❞

NOEL (2000)

❝If I could sum it up, she became more heavy metal and I became more of a hippy.❞ NOEL (TALKING ABOUT HIS SPLIT WITH MEG) (2000)

NOEL AND MEG

"I just walked straight past Meg when I saw her in court. That woman has taken me to court and I abhor it. It is all so unnecessary. But if somebody wants their pound of flesh that badly, there is nothing you can do to stop it. If it means that much to her that she is going to drag me through the courts and have our lives splashed all over the newspapers again because she can't keep her mouth shut, then fine. Fuck it." **NOEL (2001)**

"**The party girls and all that shite. Grow up and get a proper job. After I had split up with Meg, some people said, 'How did you end up with that lot? Everybody hates them in London.' Well, I don't particularly like them, but I don't hate anyone.**" NOEL (2001)

"Meg hated Liam and I was always trying to please her but I didn't get on with him myself, anyway. Meg and Patsy didn't get on. It was a vicious nightmare." **NOEL (2001)**

MARRIED WITH CHILDREN

❝No such thing as happily married. If you wanna see the opposite sex sprout four heads, then exchange a couple of rings. You walk to the altar with a woman with one head and you walk back up with a fucking monster. I'd much rather live with someone and have them as a girlfriend.❞ LIAM (2002)

❝Marriage is a ridiculous concept. I hate people who say, 'Oh, I've found my soulmate.' That's bullshit. There's only one soulmate and that's the man upstairs. I don't even know why I bothered getting married in the first place – a moment of fucking weakness, as well as an amazing tax fiddle. You can save loads of money from the tax man, but you end up paying it back in spades at the other end of the marriage.❞ LIAM (2002)

❝I was forced into it. No, it wasn't an arranged marriage (to Patsy Kensit), more a deranged marriage.❞ LIAM (2002)

❝For the record I got divorced 'cos it was the right thing for me then and it is now. There's no big fucking sinister conspiracy. I haven't got any bad blood towards my ex. I've had a great life. Really, I have. I'm grateful. It's just it got to the point when there was nothing more for me to say to her, nothing more for her say to me, so I said, 'I'm off.' We only speak when it's to do with (daughter) Anaïs. That's it. Other than that, it's gone.❞ NOEL (2002)

❝I'd had a shitty year. Just come off tour. Missus had left. I ain't fucking Superman. I came home, she's fucked off and left me with a tea bag. I went on the piss. End of story.❞ LIAM (2002)

❝As soon as Noel got divorced from his missus and as soon as I got divorced we got on better. It wasn't just those two, it was their crowd. They're so rude and they've got no soul. They're a bunch of parasites.❞ LIAM (2002)

Fatherhood

"There's so much stigma attached to being estranged from your kid that, for a while, I beat myself up over it. I'd see Anaïs and want it to be so special that... well, you forget that all kids of that age are interested in is drawing on walls and throwing cakes around the fucking room. When it comes to the point when I can communicate with my daughter properly, I'll sit her down and say, 'This is what happened. These were the reasons... Until then, I'll continue to chase her round the room with a funny mask on!'" NOEL (2001)

"I see her (daughter Anaïs) every other weekend, and every Thursday and Friday on the alternate weeks." **NOEL (2001)**

"I'm not naturally a great father, but I'm getting better. I can spend hours with Anaïs, I can spend whole days letting her ride around on my back." NOEL (2001)

MARRIED WITH CHILDREN

"She (Anaïs) is the spitting image of me, which is not a good thing for a little girl. Obviously, I am not going to be with her day to day for the rest of her life, so let's hope that Meg can raise a pretty decent human being.**"** NOEL (2001)

"There are not that many things that I haven't done in my 34 years. There are not many places I haven't been. I have cried a lot of tears and laughed a lot of laughs. I've had to make some tough decisions and I have become pretty worldly in the process. But I am infuriatingly rational and, for the child that I have and the children that I hope to have, I want to be a good and approachable father." NOEL (2001)

LIAM AND NICOLE APPLETON

"How has life changed since (son) Lennon was born? I'm probably still in shock, 'cos he's just a baby at the moment. I suppose he has changed my life, but not as in cleaned it... He's just made me aware that I can't be what I used to be. I packed in the booze for a start, and I am a bit nicer. I'm nice round him. I've always been a nice person, you know. I have bad days, but I've always been a pleasant kind of guy.

"I got a call saying I gotta go to the hospital and I was like, 'Fucking hell' and she was there, having these pains and that stuff. And then (the doctor) goes, 'Right, get your gear on.' I was like, 'Oh, what gear?' The hospital clothes! I was shitting it, actually. But it was good. I was there at the birth.**"** LIAM (2000)

❝ I'm happy with it (his relationship with son Lennon), Patsy's happy, the kid's happy that's all that matters. We still speak, I don't hate her, the kid's the best thing that's ever happened to me. So everything's cool. ❞

LIAM (2001)

❝ I've gotta go an' blow some balloons up, me! Blowing balloons up, fookin' dressed up as Postman Pat. Fooking pure rock'n'roll. ❞

LIAM (2001) PREPARING FOR SON'S BIRTHDAY PARTY

❝ Liam is the life and soul of the party. I probably always stand in the kitchen. Like the other day Liam's son had his second birthday party. I'm not one for sitting round with party hats on me head, I'm more like a grumpy uncle, whereas Liam is there with his face painted and he's dressing up for the kids and stuff. ❞

NOEL (2001)

❝ He (Liam) is a fantastic dad. He and his little boy are like best mates. I wish I could be like that but I think I will come into my own when my kids are teenagers. I'll be able to give them good advice about what to do land stuff. ❞ **NOEL (2001)**

❝ I don't have to deal with her (Patsy). I see my son (Lennon) every week, I'll tell her what's going on. And I have to make sure she gets her money, which pisses me off – but that's life. ❞ LIAM (2002)

❝ I'm still a crackhead... No, after a couple of kids I've changed. ❞

LIAM (2002)

❝ She (Anaïs) likes us (Oasis). Her favourite song is 'Stop Crying Your Heart Out.' ❞ NOEL (2002)

❝ I'm 30 in September. I don't want my kids to see their pissed-up madhead dad down the pub. I've got responsibilities, but occasionally I wanna rock with the best of them. ❞ **LIAM (2002)**

MARRIED WITH CHILDREN

"On fatherhood: Love it. Really good at it. Wait 'til you see my two kids at 20, they're going to be causing chaos, man. You have to dig deep. You have to teach them things you never learnt yourself. I'm always saying, 'Fucking get out of there!' And then I tell myself, 'Why can't you talk to yourself like this from time to time?' That would keep me out of scrapes." LIAM (2002)

LIAM AND NICOLE

"The day Anaïs turns round to me and says, 'Drugs is like having a cup of tea in the morning,' I'll have to deal with it. What will I do? Lock her in her room for six months? No. You say, 'Life is like this. You make your choices. And love them.' That's all you can do."

NOEL (2002)

"Nic probably wants some (children) but I've got two... I want to concentrate on what I've got for now." LIAM (2002)

"She'll (Anaïs) have the best education money can buy. I don't want her turning round at 16 and saying, 'Oi you cunt, I've just read the press cuttings. You're minted! Why did you send me to a comprehensive in Lambeth, you tight bastard!?' I want her to be Prime Minister. And you have to go to a posh school for that."

NOEL (2002)

Changing Partners

"My private life is good at the moment partly because of Sara, and partly because I've got out of that celebrity thing. Having spent far too long worrying about what fucking party I was going to attend, I'm now concentrating on the day-to-day living of life." NOEL (2001)

NOEL AND GIRLFRIEND SARA McDONALD

"I found she was as sarcastic towards me as I am to her (new girlfriend Sara). It's there and it's happening so let's just enjoy it for what it is. Why analyse what's right? You just analyse the life out of things. Just do it man. It's like the world's about to go to fucking war, you know, let it go."

NOEL (2001)

"I sit and laugh, just thinking about how she (Sara McDonald) makes me laugh." NOEL (2001)

MARRIED WITH CHILDREN

❝I'd be fookin' mad to be thinking about getting married; I've only just been divorced. But Nicole (Appleton)'s fooking great; she's right up my street.❞ **LIAM (2001)**

❝**Two years ago, maybe the band wasn't that important, but the reason the band's stayed together is 'cos it has to, because basically I've got fuck all else... in my life. The group, me little daughter and me girlfriend... that pretty much rounds it all off for me. Haven't got anything else to look forward to.**❞ NOEL (2001)

❝Nicky (Nicole Appleton) loves him, she actually adores him and he adores her. He is just a joy to be around at the moment. So now that Liam's with Nicky and I'm with Sara, we go out in a foursome for Sunday lunch and stuff like that. And we have the funniest, funniest times, which we never did before. I don't know if it is a cliché or not, but behind these two very happy brothers are two very good ladies.❞ **NOEL (2001)**

❝**It was easier than having a tattoo. The baby doesn't look like anyone yet, but Nicky looks great. She doesn't look like she has just had a baby. She looks relaxed like she's just been shopping.**❞ NOEL ON THE ARRIVAL OF LIAM AND NICOLE'S BABY SON, GENE (2001)

❝I fancied Nicole when I first saw her, which was in France. Then, when I hung out with her I thought, 'You're fun.' We could get pissed together. She was like a mate. Nic likes a drink, she likes the pub. My ex-missus never saw the inside of a pub in her life. She thought she was fucking Elizabeth Taylor. I'd say 'You coming down the pub?' She'd turn her nose up and go, 'The pub? Pubs are shit!' Well they're great in my world.❞ **LIAM (2002)**

❝**Nic's like a little scally bird. She doesn't walk around in fucking Gucci every fucking minute of the day... At the end of the day they all stink and fart when you're next to 'em in bed in the morning.**❞

LIAM (2002)

“The difference is Nic's not a professional Oasis girlfriend.”

NOEL (2002)

“I don't know about soul mate, but she's (Nicole) definitely my best mate. She's cool and I don't want to fuck it up with her and that's it.” LIAM (2003)

“I think I'm romantic, but my girlfriend (Sara) insists that I am the most unromantic person of my generation.” NOEL (2005)

“She's perfect, Nicole. She's the one. And, by rights, I should marry her if she'd have me, but I am still a bit dubious.”

LIAM (2002)

NICOLE AND LIAM WITH BABY GENE

MARRIED WITH CHILDREN

Larging It

Drugs

"Tricky was saying we should be doing some stuff together. I said, 'Sure, if you've got the stuff, I've got the razor blade and mirror'. But he meant music, unfortunately." **NOEL (1995)**

"I went to my doctor and said, 'Can I get some Prozac?' And he went, 'No, fuck off.'" NOEL (1995)

"Nobody in Oasis has ever done heroin, crack, acid or any form of downers or anything that makes you lose the marbles big time. Most of the band get stoned, we all get pissed, we all do E every now and again. We're not as mad as people make us out to be.

If I ever found that anybody in the band was doing heroin or any form of heroin substitute they would get sacked on the spot. Immediately.

"The thing that pisses me off about talking about this is when people read it they say, 'Oh, they boast about their drug intake.' But if people ask us a question we won't sit here and lie, like 90 per cent of the bands." **NOEL (1995)**

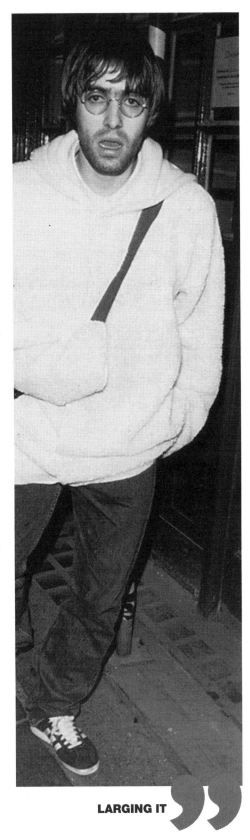

"Whoever said I'm on a line of cocaine every 40 minutes, I'll sue the fucker. That's out of order. Me and our Liam will take anything that's put in front of us because... that's just the kind of guys we are. But we've never been on stage out of it. We've never taken heroin or crack.

"We do take too many drugs, though, and I wish I'd never started. In fact, I wish I'd never started smoking cigarettes or drinking beer or taking cocaine or ecstasy because I'd have a lot more money. The thing about us is we're honest. If we're asked whether we take drugs, we say yes. I was brought up by my mam not to be a liar." NOEL (1996)

"I'm not an addict. In fact, before tonight I've not even had a drink or any drugs for a week while I've been in Europe. It's a psychological dependence. When you're young and on the dole and got no money, sometimes all you're left with is your snidey fucking drug deal. For five quid every weekend you can maybe escape the place you're in. Then that becomes the norm.

"Our mam has been trying to deal with her sons' drug habits for 10 years. She took us to the brink of adulthood and in the end she threw her hands up. She said, 'This is left, this is right, this is black, this is white, this is wrong, this is right. If you don't accept that, fuck you'. NOEL (1996)

LARGING IT

"When I wasn't on drugs I was going to get them or coming back from getting them. I remember sitting in my house and a party started on a Friday afternoon and it went through 'til Monday, and I'm still meeting people to this day who were there and I don't recognise them. I mean proper minging shady-looking characters I would back away from in the streets." NOEL (2001)

"I'm not very good at sitting around a dinner table with people and discussing the day's events on Sky News. Between '94 and '98, I was in a different state of mind. I was social because I was taking a lot of drugs. A lot of party drugs as well. I didn't smoke spliff or take heroin. It was the drugs that make you wanna go out.**"**

NOEL (2001)

"I liked drugs, I was good at them. But I'd had panic attacks for about a year and I stopped because I wanted to. After you make the decision, it is quite easy. And I am quite proud of the fact that I didn't have to check into one of those dodgy clinics and have someone tell me I was a bad person. Because I am not."

NOEL (2001)

"From 1993 to when I stopped taking drugs on June 5, 1998, I can hardly remember a thing,**" NOEL (2001)**

"I can remember signing our first record deal. I don't remember recording our album, *(What's The Story) Morning Glory*. I was deranged. I don't particularly remember getting married. Not at all. Not that I would want to remember it." NOEL (2001)

"I've calmed down a bit. I don't do them (drugs) every day and night. And I don't do them around people who aren't interested. The days I do them I wake up and look in the mirror and think, 'You dick!' It fucks up my routine which is; get up at 7am, bed at 10pm. If I'm still shit-faced when I come round at 10 in the morning I think. 'You twat!'**" LIAM (2002)**

LARGING IT

❝I stopped doing drugs and people slowly noticed – there was no big meeting. We're not a bunch of Christians. I didn't start dressing orange net curtains and shaving my head and banging a tambourine. I stopped because doing coke with seven other geezers on a tour bus over several months is bad for the soul. You say things you don't mean and some of the things you say are so outrageous you can never take them back.❞ NOEL (2002)

LIAM, GEM, NOEL AND ANDY

❝I did a few lines Saturday night. I put a rocket up everyone. Shooting my gob off. I've got a lot of making up to do.❞ LIAM (2002)

❝I went to the kitchen, straight out of bed, hair all over the place, got a can of lager out the fridge, chopped a fucking line out and at that point I thought, 'What am I fucking doing?' I worked myself into such a fucking state that I just phoned the doctor and said, 'Please man, give me something,' and he said 'I can't give you anything, just fucking stop doing it.' From that day I never touched drugs.❞ NOEL (2002)

“Can you imagine walking through the Priory (hospital) and seeing Robbie Williams coming over, say, in a fucking dressing gown? That's enough to drive you to heroin!” **NOEL (2002)**

Drink

“I don't think I've ever had a drink problem. I just like to drink. I could give it up like that, but who am I giving it up for? For some other cunt? If you don't wanna drink, then don't drink. If you wanna do summat, do it. I drink 'cos I want to. Not because I need to. It's like, if some shit goes on I don't go 'Oh fuck, I need a drink'. There's no booze in my house. If I was a big heavy fucking drinker, which all these idiots think I am, there'd be beer in my house. It's full of water, my house, and the only time I have a drink is when I go to the pub. Our kid reckons I shouldn't drink. Y'know, I reckon there's a lot of things he shouldn't do.” **LIAM (2000)**

“**When I drink, I drink. I don't fookin' pussy about. I get stuck in there and get wasted and I like it and I wake up the next day and think 'fookin' hell' then I leave off for a bit. I'm quite happy with my drinking situation at the moment.**” LIAM (2001)

"I was off the booze, man, so I just drank loads of water and was in the bog all the time pissing. I was chilling. I wrote a couple of songs out there, it was good. I learned a few bits that I'd been struggling with.**"** **LIAM (2001)**

"No drugs, man. I've had enough. For the time being. I've not given up, but (yawns) I just can't be bothered. Got too much shit going on in my life to be snorting gear. I've got a kid to look after, I've gotta be strong. But you can't give up fuckin' booze, man. A couple of pints is okay. And I have a lot of pints, I can drink for England, but you can only drink so much before you're asleep."

LIAM (2000)

"We all go out and get drunk and don't even fight anymore.**"** **NOEL (2001)**

"I can drink like a god but I'm pukin' up a lot these days."

LIAM (2002)

"We're going out a lot as a band the moment and that's great. And if I wasn't in a band I'd be doing it anyway. Probably worse, because there wouldn't some cunt waiting for me to take my photo and put me in the papers the next morning.**"** **LIAM (2002)**

"I don't really know what we're going to do about his (Liam's) drinking and behaviour – we've been here before but I really don't want to be here again." NOEL (2002)

Rock'n'Roll Star...
The Music

❝I think American youth has had enough of people telling them how crap their lives are and I think that when they listen to our records we just tell them how good their lives could be. People like Eddie Vedder... what's the point? Why's he in a band if he's so pissed off with it? Why doesn't he go work in a car wash or McDonalds?**❞**

NOEL (1995)

❝Rock'n'roll is about music. Music. Music. Music. It's not about you, it's not about me, it's not about Oasis. It's about the songs.❞

NOEL (1994)

❝We pity anybody who doesn't buy our records.**❞** **LIAM (1994)**

❝We're not part of all this. We're more important than some stupid industry circus.❞ NOEL (1994) IN NEW YORK DURING THE NEW MUSIC SEMINAR

❝It's the amount we sell that's important, not the chart positions. I mean when The Jam put out singles they were selling far more than bands do now. They'd go straight in at Number 1 then drop out a week later. These days someone like Take That sell hardly any and they're still Number 1 for months. In a couple of years time it'll be like 20 years since the first Jam single. I'd like us to be able to put across some of the spirit of those days, the sense of things being special.**❞** **NOEL (1994)**

❝The thing is, there'll always be people who are into lads getting on a stage and playing the best music in the world. It's always going to happen, innit? I mean, we've yet to see the next Beatles...❞ LIAM (1994)

OASIS *Talking*

❝I think acid music's naff, me. It depends what you call dance music. Sly & The Family Stone is dance music... Sly Stone is good music, right. But all this dance music these days is all that same silly beat going DANK DANK DANK, and you sit there and have a cup of tea, and it's going DANK DANK DANK. I've got to slag it right off. It's doing my head in.❞ LIAM (1994)

❝**If I go and see a band, right, I don't wanna see some daft act with a fuckin' dance routine or summat. It's all just about getting on there, straight, bang, music, in your face, and nothing else. It's dead obvious. It ain't hard to work it out.**❞ LIAM (1994)

❝We're the future of music, never mind just rock, pal. I hope someone comes along and tries to take our crown, though – it'd be nice to have a bit of competition. If we're meant to be the new Beatles then where are the new Stones and the new Who?❞

LIAM (1995)

❝**I've been to lots of gigs recently and they've all been pretty fuckin' average. I saw Gene 'cos I had fuck all else to do. They**

were all right. But Suede are shit and I fuckin' hate them. And Elastica. And Echobelly. And Menswear. I want to stop slagging other bands off 'cos I've met most of them now and they're really nice people. But I have to be honest and say that they're not very good.❞ NOEL (1995)

❝I don't want people watching me and thinking 'I could do that'. I want them thinking they could never do that.❞ **NOEL (1995)**

"All my mates are into the fucking Chemical Brothers. I hate it. Non-imaginative bollocks keyboard crap. If a new reggae band come up, they don't get slated. No one says, 'You're retro.' It's just reggae music. But if you're going rock'n'roll, everyone says that you're living in the past. Rock'n'roll will never die. It will get done by other people, like me and Bonehead, but rock'n'roll will never die. So why slag them off for wanting to pick up a guitar, when you're not slagging the man off for doing reggae?" LIAM (1996)

"I don't listen to many of these late-Nineties bands. I still listen to Elvis, you know. We write songs on electric guitars and amplifiers. We don't follow trends or fashions. We're probably one of the two rock'n'roll bands left on the road. It's Oasis and Black Crowes. We do what we do. And we want to keep going, in the traditional sense. We want to secure our own identity. We don't do jazz, salsa or reggae. We're a rock band." NOEL (2000)

"We don't need to prove anything to anyone. At the end of the day you can go to a Radiohead show and stroke your fucking beard and watch the miserable cunt complaining, or come see us, put your arm round your best mate and have it." NOEL (2002)

"Is anyone making mind-bending music anymore? We're a rock'n'roll group. We're not fucking Blur.**"**

NOEL (2002)

"We're not fucking wizards. We're four blokes from Manchester who happen to be the best band in the world." LIAM (2002)

"If I can't feel the wind from the amps making my trousers flap, then I'd rather go fucking shopping.**" NOEL (2002)**

"I don't think he (Liam) sounds like Lennon at all. I think he sounds more like Johnny Rotten."

NOEL (2002)

Wibbling Rivalry...
Noel & Liam

"I live with the guy, and that's what he is. He's a fucking slob. Ask me mam." **NOEL ON LIAM (1994)**

"Our kid tends to take everything fuckin' literally. He's a bit of a cosmic guy, a bit up in the sky. He believes in spirituality and all that. I believe in black and white." NOEL (1994)

"Liam's as good a singer as I am, but I can only sing acoustically. It's cool with me. He sings the way I want him to. I can't fault him. I don't think I'd let anyone else do it if it wasn't him." **NOEL (1994)**

"I tell you, when I read that Oasis is Noel's band, that really fuckin' sent me... It's no-one's band. It's all of us. Take one away and there's nowt left." LIAM (1994)

"I fuckin' hate that twat there. I fuckin' hate him. And I hope one day there's a release where I can smash fuck out of him, with a fuckin' Rickenbacker, right on his nose, and then he does the same to me, 'cos I think we're stepping right up to it now. There's a fuckin' line there, and we're right on the edge of it." **LIAM (1994)**

"I win nearly all of our fights. He's caused me a bit of harm, but that's about it. Big brothers are supposed to be harder, but he's chilled out and I'm not. He's seen a lot of things I haven't. I'm more of a nutter, I've got more aggression. We don't fight as much as we used to. We chatted about it months ago and decided to cool down a bit." LIAM (1995)

OASIS *Talking*

❝I don't think we've ever fought any more than any other brothers. That's just a press thing. I have to say I don't think his voice is a good as it was a year ago, but that's just because we've all been working so hard. We need a rest soon.**❞** NOEL (1995)

❝I haven't a clue what makes Liam tick. I think he's at war with the world, but I'm not sure why. There's something really getting to him, but I don't know what it is. He's always questioning everything, looking for answers. I think life's just a load of questions. If I don't find the answers now, then fuck it, I'm sure they'll turn up later on. Our kid doesn't want that, he wants to know all the answers right now.❞ NOEL (1995)

❝People say we're always fighting...(but) I'm just standing up for myself and he's getting the idea that it's his band and we're all supposed to be sheep. The rest of them all go along with it, but I'm not going to. I mean, if he told them all to turn up tomorrow because he'd got a plan that we were going to play a gig up a lamp post, they'd all just do it. I'd have asked, 'Why are we playing up a lamp post? Can't we play a stadium or something?'**❞** LIAM (1995)

❝I said to him yesterday, 'If I suddenly wrote something as good as "Hey Jude", I know it's not likely, but if I did, would you let us record it?' and he went, 'No, I'd quit.' And it really hurt when he said that. I know he writes brilliant songs, but I don't think he should just dismiss my ideas. When we were doing one

NOEL & LIAM **❞**

song live on the last tour. I had an idea for backing vocals on it, but when I told him he just said, 'No, that's shit'. Then when we started doing it, he started singing exactly the backing vocals I'd suggested. Then he said, 'No, they were different.' He's just too proud to admit I'm right sometimes.** LIAM (1995)

Liam's got more stupid. When he was at school, he was quite normal. Now he's definitely mad. He's not mad like some people in bands are mad. He's madder than mad... He's just mad. **NOEL (1995)**

If we weren't in a band, we'd be having rows in the house. If we had a greengrocers, Gallagher's Greengrocers, we'd argue over which way to set out the apples or pears. LIAM (1995)

"When I was 15, he was 10. A social life with him was inconceivable. It's laughable to think I'd end up in a band with him. But here we are. I'm 28 and he's 23. Such is life. When I'm 65 he'll be 60 and it'll be irrelevant, we'll both be old together." NOEL (1996)

"Liam's a fucking brilliant frontman and he stamps his authority over everything he sings. It's his. I can't even come close. Now, the way it's going is there are certain songs where I'll go, 'You're too punk-rock for this one,' so I do it. He's cool about it." NOEL (1996)

"He (Liam) already is a casualty. I don't fear for him at all. He can look after himself, I think. I hope." NOEL (1997)

"He's (Liam) crap with adults but give him a kid to play with, and he's a big softie. I'm not good at accepting people being nice to me. For instance, I'd go out of my way to hide my birthday. Sentimental family stuff tends to embarrass me – my failing, not theirs." NOEL (2001)

"I'd literally kick in his arse. I can't be rational with that boy (Liam). I'm either really placid with him or relieve him of a couple of teeth." NOEL (2001)

"He's (Liam) getting on my fucking nerves at the moment. I hate not being able to go to my own studio because he won't sing when I'm there because it freaks him out. It's just like fuck off. You know, either sing or don't sing, but don't do some fucking pastiche of the two. 'I think I might sing today, but I think I'm not in a good mood.' It's like, who do you think you are? Jim Morrison? You're meant to be an untortured artist. Either shit or get off the bog, man." NOEL (2001)

"Liam thinks he's the new John Lennon. He thinks he's fantastic. But who's gonna tell him? The same way, who's going to say to me that maybe a song's not going to be good enough?" NOEL (2001)

NOEL & LIAM

"It's good now, man. Liam's calmed down a lot, you know, he's happy with Nic, got a kid on the way - everyone's grown up a bit. Trouble is, shit happens when you've got three days off in somewhere like Albuquerque. You're in a bar on a Wednesday afternoon and someone'll say, 'I don't like that jacket' and you're like, 'What, are you calling my jacket a poof?' And you've got nothing better to do, so you start picking arguments with people. When he ain't drinking and he's not being a cunt it just makes it easier for everyone else to just do their shit, just get on with it and have a good time...' NOEL (2001)

"To Liam's eternal fucking credit, he carried it off and saved me a whole load of shit with the lawyers. I was actually fucking quite proud of him - it was good for Liam that he could actually go out and do it." **NOEL (2001) ON LIAM FRONTING THE TOUR ALONE.**

"Liam used to really annoy me, but now I think he is a comic genius, the funniest guy I have known in my entire life."
NOEL (2001)

"I think he'll (go solo) before I will. He's got more songs, and he's a lot more driven in that department, because although he's 30-odd, he's only just started writing songs." **NOEL (2005)**

"I've never heard Liam have a good word to say about any one person in his *entire life*." NOEL (2005)

"There's no point (doing a solo record) now. See, that was said around the time of the last tour. Liam was on my case 24 hours a day, he was doing my head in. Bonehead and Guigsy had left. Creation had collapsed and it was like, 'Well, is there any fucking future?'" **NOEL (2002)**

"We're not mates. We just don't feel like it. We get on better when we don't see each other and don't speak to each other so let's not be mates." LIAM (2003)

"He'd (Liam) been whingeing about his monitors all the way through the tour (Japan) and it got to the fourth song, and I just said to him off mic, 'Are you gonna fuckin' shut up for the rest of the fuckin' year or are you fuckin' gonna carry on moaning, you moaning bastard?' and he looked at me really weird and threw his tambourine on the floor like a woman and walked off." NOEL (2002)

"He's my brother – I don't have to get on with him, I don't have to like him and I don't have to dislike him because he's my family so he's always going to be there." NOEL (2003)

"If I speak to him (Liam) I'd probably knock him out...**"**

NOEL (2002)

"If he ever has any aspirations to pick up a Telecaster on stage I'll walk off. Tambourine and sunglasses. That's all you're having in your hands. You're not playing guitar in my band."

NOEL (2002)

"I can read. I just can't be bothered – I prefer to look at the pictures." LIAM (2002)

"Me and Noel are not a patch on these two (Nicole and Natalie Appleton). We fight and stuff but they're at it every two seconds." LIAM (2002)

"We had to touch the bottom for it to get better. It had to be fucking totally shit first. Plus, we had to give you lot something to write about or you'd be stuck with Travis and Coldplay and people who want a long prosperous career being nice. That ain't real. Fighting and arguing and fucking people off is real.**"** LIAM (2002)

"I can handle Liam now 'cos I'm more tolerant. I used to think, I'm the boss, so fuck off. Also, I do really mean it when I say he'll be the best songwriter in the country in five years' time. People thought I was being ironic. I wasn't, his new songs are great."

NOEL (2002)

NOEL & **LIAM** **"**

The Famous Five...
Noel & Liam
On Oasis

GUIGSY

❝There's no point in interviewing them, they've got fuck all to say for themselves, anyway.**❞**

NOEL ON BAND MEMBERS OTHER THAN LIAM (1994)

❝I've always sung me cock off, y'know, round my gaff. I'm double loud now. My style is banging it out.❞ LIAM (1994)

❝I've got a mike stand, right, and that's what I'm into, what I'm about. I'm not going to fuck off because he thinks my views are too outrageous, or whatever. I've got my vibe, and I go to that mike stand, and I do my business. Noel stands in his fuckin' corner, he does his little riffs and his little dance – let him do that. Guigsy does his bit, I'll do my bit, the drummer does his bit. That's what it's all about. Five people, not one.**❞ LIAM (1994)**

❝I don't mind our kid playing with someone else, as long as they're cool. Weller's all right 'cos he's a geezer. Maybe I'll sing with someone else. Who? I don't know. I'd sing with Weller. Or John Lennon....Yeah, I do know he's dead.❞ LIAM (1995)

❝ A lot of people think we're five people who go around being miserable all the time. But being in a band with Bonehead is not miserable, 'cos that guy is like Peter Sellers and Rigsby combined, with less morals than either of them – he's just outrageous. **❞**

NOEL (1995)

❝ He does it all in one fucking take, do you know what I mean? Alan White, he's all right – as he's now known. ❞ NOEL (1995)

❝ 'Oasis exist as a unit'. Do they fuck, man! Everyone's dispensable! Too fucking right, might even fire meself one of these days. **❞ NOEL (1995)**

ALAN WHITE

❝ If I hadn't had the songs, they'd probably have told me to fuck off. I remember playing 'Live Forever' to them on an acoustic guitar one night, and it's one of the greatest moments I've ever had as a songwriter. They were just completely and utterly fucking speechless. ❞ NOEL ON TAKING OVER THE BAND (1996)

❝ It's not just me and Noel. We're just two brothers in a fucking band, I just happen to be the singer, he happens to be the songwriter, I happen to be good-looking, he just happens to be a good songwriter, that is all it is. The other three guys are still as important. So we just went on and done it. I know what I'm fucking doing, Whitey knows what he's doing, Gem and Andy know what they're doing, we're not dickheads. We just didn't have Noel Gallagher there. It was nothing to do with me, it's to do with the spirit that is around Oasis - and the spirit around Oasis is a bit of a lunatic. He's the dog's bollocks when he wants to be. He's a nutter. **❞** LIAM (2001)

NOEL & LIAM ON OASIS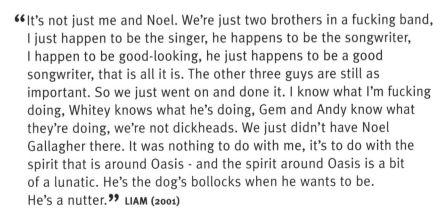

❝I'm Jack, our kid's Vera. Alan's fookin' Beppe from *Eastenders*. Gem's Boycie from *Only Fools and Horses* and Andy Bell's fookin' Neil from the *Young Ones*.❞ LIAM (2002)

GEM, LIAM, NOEL AND ANDY

❝I don't need the adulation or the fame. But we'll keep going for a long time I would have thought.❞ **NOEL (2003)**

❝We are geniuses. Musical history is simply Elvis Presley, The Beatles, The Sex Pistols and Oasis.❞ LIAM (2002)

❝How close did we come to splitting? We didn't. We sat down and I said, 'Listen, I love you and you love me, what's the most important thing? One: the music. Two: the singer. Three: the cunt who writes the songs.' So we got rid of the fucking entourage of 450 cunts hanging around us, he (Liam) cut down on his drinking and wrote some fantastic songs, we got working with two great musicians and here we are.❞ **NOEL (2002)**

Champagne Supernovas... Wealth & Fame

“When I saw The Stone Roses, I just thought, I could do that. And I did, didn't I?” **NOEL (1994)**

“People never ask me for my autograph. They think I look too grumpy to approach. What they don't understand is that I always look like this. Of course I have my good days and my bad days. Sometimes, like tonight, I'll think: 'Fuck this, man. I can't be arsed with all the bullshit nonsense.'” NOEL (1994)

“I've got about ten guitars. I don't need them, I don't even use them. It's just that whenever I see a guitar that I really like, I have to have it. I guess I'm a bit like Imelda Marcos was with shoes.”
NOEL (1994)

“I'm not in the band to fuck about. I'm in it for the music because I love music and I love writing songs, but I'm in it for the money as well. What I want is a car, but I can't drive and I don't want to, so I want someone to drive me around and I don't want any fuckin' hassle off anyone. Then, when I decide to call it a day, I'd like nobody to know where I was.” NOEL (1994)

“Crazy Horse love our band, right? That stands us apart from every fucking Shed Seven, Radiohead, Echobelly – all that shit that's here today gone tomorrow. I can go and play with the legends and not be out of my depth. We're respected by Paul Weller. You won't see Thom from fucking Radiohead playing with the Velvet fucking Underground or whatever.”
NOEL ON JAMMING ONSTAGE WITH NEIL YOUNG'S BACKING BAND (1994)

OASIS *Talking*

“Creation doesn't pay us enough money. That's why I got kicked out of my flat. Last Sunday was my 27th birthday and d'you know how I spent it? In bed in a tiny hotel room, on my own with the phone off the hook. No wonder I'm depressed.” NOEL (1994)

“I was walking around Oxford Street today, and I had to do four photographs and maybe a dozen autographs just for passers-by. This time last year I would have still done them but I would have been paranoid that people were walking past going, 'Look at that knobhead'. I don't give a fuck about that anymore. Now I'd happily stand there and do an autograph or a photograph for anyone.**”**

NOEL (1995)

“The advantages are that if you're the songwriter you earn the most money. If you're a band member then you earn a living, no more and no less.” NOEL (1995)

“It's the same thing we did in England before the first single came out. We'd play support to anybody and it was worth it just for the buzz of getting an audience in the palm of our hand. Two songs and we could show anyone how good we were. Now we're doing that in America... we don't need all that bullshit about meeting the head of promotions or whatever.**” NOEL (1995)**

❝I hardly ever get recognised. Or, if I do then it's always some kid who comes up to me and goes, 'Hey, are you Noel from Oasis?' And if I say, 'Yeah', they always go, 'No, you're not.' They always seem to think I'm someone who just looks like me. I should get a T-shirt that says, 'Yes It Is, Really.' All this celebrity thing is just fucking weird.❞ NOEL (1995)

❝Right now there isn't a band in the world as good as us and they know it.❞ LIAM (1995)

❝The main thing is that although the royalties on the records are split five ways, I'm the songwriter and I get the publishing. It's not a source of conflict. Whether they're jealous or not, you'd have to ask them. They've never said anything to me. I can't believe they'd expect a share of my songs.❞ NOEL (1996)

❝Yes I do feel under pressure. But it's only internal pressure because of the standards that I set, it's nobody else that puts me under pressure. I don't give a fuck if anybody likes it, I don't care it if gets slagged off. That's not why I'm in it. Any journalist can pick holes in the new record if they like but the thing is that it won't come out of the studio if I'm not happy with it. Once it's in the shops you can slag it off then because that's what people do, innit?❞ NOEL (1995)

❝I've already made a name for myself. I'm using the band to live a better life.❞ NOEL (1996)

❝People think we're some sort of superhuman beings who can sail through life. But I get down. I've cried about some of the things that have happened to me but not when people are around. I've lost a lot of friends. I've split up with my girlfriend who I was with for six years. I've lost that and I don't think I'll ever get over it.❞

NOEL (1994)

WEALTH & FAME

"Whatever you do, people are going to get pissed off. I came back on the train the other day and I was sitting in the smoking compartment in second class talking to someone, having a good conversation. And this woman, with like, 23 children or something came up and told me I shouldn't be taking up the seat. She goes, 'You're a pop star, you should go and sit in first class.' And if I'd gone and sat in first class, people would have been saying, 'Who does he think he is? Does he think he's better than us?' or something." LIAM (1995)

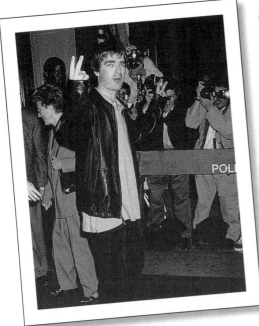

"We have the tabloids outside my flat and they go through my dustbins. We know there's a geezer who stands outside with a radio scanner, scanning the calls.

"But you have to deal with it. You know; deny nothing, man, because I've got nothing to be ashamed of. I don't think anyone could do an exposé of anything that we've ever done because everybody knows fucking who and what we are and what we do, so, if they can't deal with it, then fuck 'em." NOEL (1996)

"Fame's bollocks. Not something I started the band for. Didn't start a band to be famous; started a band to play good music. Some of fame's fun, some of it's not fun. Ya know, people slagging you off, people giving you grief because they don't like your music. Little bits and bobs. It's 50-50." LIAM (1996)

❝I don't go through a lot of pressure or pain , although when you get famous and wealthy and you're Irish and you're Catholic and you're working class you do carry that guilt for life. But if I've got problems, then they'll remain mine and nobody else's.❞ NOEL (1996)

❝**You can't be in a big famous rock band and not have that. It'd be quite bizarre to be in a big band and not have journalists following you around.**❞ LIAM (1999)

❝We were running out of money, had to write a new album to get a few quid when we had all these fucking tax bills to pay. Ridiculous. I could do with a few more pairs of shoes.❞ LIAM (1997)

❝**I'm going to live in Ireland. But not for tax purposes. That's for greedy cunts. I like the taxman. The taxman's good. Fuck it. And anyway, England's good. It's full of people walking the streets like me.**❞ LIAM (1997)

"I'm up for lamping people, but not these days. You can lamp 'em when you've got no money, but when you've fucking got loads of money you can't lamp 'em 'cos they sue you." **LIAM (1997)**

"I've never been one for donating large amounts of money to charity because I donate a lot of money as it is. It's called forty fucking per cent tax." NOEL (2001)

"I've been to the top of the mountain and I've seen the view and being in the biggest band is great because of the adulation and the money and the fucking flying around in jets. But it's a lot of work to keep it going though, man." **NOEL (2001)**

"I fookin' love being famous, me. I fookin' love it, I love it I LOOOVE IT!!! Well, I thought it would've backed off by now, but obviously there's no-one else a bit more interesting than us to write about so they keep doin' it. The pop lot, right, their goal in life is to have their picture took. Soon as someone goes, 'You're that geezer out of such and such,' - boomf! - they're in heaven."

LIAM (2001)

"If people start mithering me , I tell them. Or switch off. Fame? What's that? It's the state of your mind." **LIAM (1997)**

"Famous or not famous, I don't give a shit. Some famous people can be complete wankers." LIAM (1997)

"I'm down to me last eight or nine million (joking about *Sun* story). Because it takes over an hour to get to the studio from where I live by car, we sometimes take the train. Ignoring the fact that there's no First Class between London and Wycombe, they concocted a story which says, 'Noel Gallagher's so broke he's travelling economy on British Rail'." **NOEL (2001)**

WEALTH & **FAME**

The Masterplan...
Heroes & Influences

Stone Roses

❝It was the first gig I ever went to. And Ian Brown came on, and he was giving it the vibe and all that...❞ LIAM (1994)

❝Liam shared a room with me for years, he didn't know what the fuck he was going on about, until The Stone Roses, and he could totally identify with Ian Brown. And I went, 'Now d'you know what I've been talking about for the past 10 years?'❞ NOEL (1994)

❝I can't explain it but when I saw the Roses on stage, it did something to me. They were real people, doing it from the heart and they just treated everything about themselves dead special, which is right.❞ LIAM (1994)

❝*Second Coming*'s better than all the rest that's around, apart from us. It's all right, but five years is a long time, y'know? And even though it's different, I don't think they're writing songs any more. It's a shame, 'cos that's what they were good at. I loved them first time around, I was a big fan. But we're better than them nowadays; and as a songwriter, our kid pees all over John Squire.❞ LIAM (1995)

Punk

❝Who do I admire? Lydon and Lennon. The two Johns. Some of Shaun Ryder's stuff was good. That's about it, innit?❞ **LIAM (1994)**

❝***Never Mind The Bollocks Here's The Sex Pistols*** **was the record that changed my life. It came out when I was 11 but I didn't actually hear it until I was about 13. I'd been playing guitar for a while, so when that came out I had to learn every riff because all the guitar parts were really easy to play.**
❝**My mum fucking hated it. Very Catholic, so she didn't really approve of tracks like 'Bodies'. It had to be really good if she didn't like it. She even used to hide the record from me, so I had to buy it on tape and hide it in my pocket.**❞ NOEL (1995)

❝Who inspired me? First it was Steve Jones with his white Les Paul and his leather kecks. But I didn't take it seriously until I saw Johnny Marr. He had the Brian Jones haircut and the shades and the white polo neck and the red semi-acoustic. When the Smiths came on *Top Of The Pops* for the first time, that was it for me. From that day on... I wanted to be Johnny Marr.❞ **NOEL (1996)**

SEX PISTOLS

Miscellaneous

"The Bee Gees. I always thought they were a load of old shite, but then someone gave me a tape of their early stuff and it's brilliant. I like getting surprised by things like that. The only people that everyone thinks I like, but which I don't are The Clash and The Beach Boys. I just can't see it."

NOEL (1994)

"Pete Townshend is my favourite member of The Who. Keith Moon was the mad one, but Peter was the man who wrote all the songs. Pete Townshend influenced Paul Weller who, in turn, influenced me." NOEL (1995)

ELVIS PRESLEY

"I was watching (Muhammad Ali bio-pic) *When We Were Kings* the other day and he just jumped in me, man. I've got a bit of Lennon... and now I've got a bit of Ali. I've got two loudmouth arrogant bastards living inside me." LIAM (1997)

"My heroes as a kid in Manchester? Paul Weller, Johnny Marr, John Lydon, John Lennon, Paul McCartney, George Harrison, Ringo Starr, Mick Jagger, Brian Jones, Jimi Hendrix, Keith Moon, Pete Townshend, Steve Jones, Chuck Berry, Elvis Presley." NOEL (1997)

"I'm lucky in that all the heroes I've met have been pretty fucking cool to me. Someone who was a right cunt to Liam, God bless him, was Johnny Lydon. We met him and his brother in LA and, as the ale flowed, he got more and more lippy. Liam - or 'the singer', as Lydon insisted on calling him - said something about being

HEROES & **INFLUENCES**

a Smiths fan and he goes, 'How can you like them? He's fucking gay, Morrissey.' Then he looked at me and went, 'Are you wearing make-up?' To which I replied, 'Piss off, you fat little bastard!' I knew that him having a pop at Morrissey was a wind-up, but our kid was ready to twat him!" NOEL (2001)

"I met (Echo & The Bunnymen's) Ian McCulloch at a gig and thought, 'Aye, aye, here's a right mouthy bollocks,' but then we clicked and spent six hours together in the bogs. Not having sex, I hasten to add." **NOEL (2001)**

Beatlemania

"I think we'll be the most important band in the fucking world. If time is on our side and there's not so much bad shit and no one dies, then we'll be the new Beatles. We'll mean just as much because Noel's written about 200 fucking songs that nobody's ever heard and everyone of them is a fucking classic. We're way ahead." LIAM (1994)

"I was terrified when I met McCartney. I didn't have anything to say. But it was good when he taught me the chords to 'Come Together'. Piece of piss. I won't be doing a duet with him, I'm too big for that now. I'm not doing that with any Tom, Dick and Harry." **NOEL (1995)**

"My favourite song by The Beatles is 'Ticket To Ride'. I don't know why I like it more than 'Strawberry Fields' – it's just a great three-minute pop song, one of the greatest ever written."

NOEL (1995)

"Lennon was probably a twat as a person. I probably wouldn't get on with him at all. In fact, I would probably have hated him but all I'm bothered about is his songs. Those songs meant a real lot to me. I don't care about songwriters, all I care about is the songs. So like, if I met Neil Young or Keith Richards or Mick Jagger tomorrow and they were really obnoxious and rude, I wouldn't stop listening to their music." **NOEL (1995)**

"That fucking Robson and Jerome record was released the same week our album went up to Number 2 and The Beatles went down to Number 3. If we'd been 1 and The Beatles had been 2 I wanted to take out an advert with those two chart positions blown up. Oasis Are Bigger Than The Beatles for a week at least. I love it." NOEL (1995)

"The drums on 'Wonderwall' come in on the word 'backbeat', which is what we wanted – a reference to The Beatles." NOEL (1995)

"Some of the lines from 'Don't Look Back In Anger' come from John Lennon. I got this tape in America that had apparently been burgled from the Dakota Hotel and someone had found these cassettes. Lennon was starting to record his memoirs on tape. He's going on about 'trying to start a revolution from me bed, because they said the brains I had went to my head.' Thank you, I'll take that." NOEL (1996)

NOEL WITH SIR PAUL McCARTNEY
AND PAUL WELLER

HEROES & **INFLUENCES**

"People say, 'I heard the Beatles when I was four.' That's bullshit. When you're four you've got a dummy in your mouth that you keep spitting out until your mum sticks it back in yer gob. Then you shit all over the place. You do this, you do that, you're not listening to Beatles records. I didn't understand what music was until I was 18." LIAM (1996)

"If I'd been born at the same time as John Lennon, I'd have been up there. Well, I'd definitely have been better than Gerry and the fucking Pacemakers, I know that.
"From what I've heard from Paul McCartney, he likes about half a dozen of my songs. I met him twice, on the *Come Together* album and then I went round his house in St John's Wood one night. He liked 'Slide Away', 'Whatever' and 'Live Forever'. If I'd been knocked over by a taxi that night, I'd have died the happiest man." NOEL (1996)

"If we were to sit down now and take John Lennon, Jimi Hendrix, Ray Davies, Steve Marriott, anybody's first two albums against my first two albums, I'm there. I'm with The Beatles. If you ask me where I'll be after my eighth album in comparison to The Beatles, then they'll piss all over me. Probably." NOEL (1996)

"George Harrison (who described Oasis as 'derivative and silly') doesn't know Liam 'cos he's never met him. And if you haven't met Liam and just read about him in the papers, I can understand why anyone wouldn't like him. But unless you get to know him, you shouldn't be making statements like that. But we all love you, George. We think you're top!" NOEL (1997)

Paul Weller

"I'd bought this acoustic guitar, a bit like an old Beatles guitar. Paul wanted to borrow it to use on his album. Then he said I might as well play on the song myself. It was a cover of Dr John's 'Walk On Gilded Splinters'. I'd never heard it before in my life, but I wasn't going to tell him that. I said, 'Yeah, love that song. What chord's it in again?' I bluffed my way through it brilliantly. At least I thought so. Then after we'd finished, Paul came up to me and said, 'You don't know that song at all, do you?'" **NOEL (1995)**

HEROES & INFLUENCES

**"I think he was born virtually the same day as I was, he's
a Gemini too, we've both got a chipped front tooth, which he sees
as a sign because McCartney's got one and he's a Gemini as well,
and we've all got blue eyes... it's a sign! It was a social thing at
first. We both live in London, I'd ring him up and say what you
doing tonight? We just gradually got to know each other better.
I had posters of him, from *Smash Hits* on my wall! So yeah, the
first few nights when I was round at his or he was round at mine
were actually quite daunting...**

**"He was curious as to what anybody actually thought of him.
It was good for him, 'cos I'm nine years younger than him. What
struck me was how aware he was of the music scene... I was
thinking, I hope I'm like that when I'm 37... He's dead upfront and
dead honest and I really haven't got a bad word to say about the
guy except he can't take his drink."** NOEL (1995)

"People think Paul Weller's some deep god, but he's a moany old
bastard. He's like Victor Meldrew with a suntan. He's a nice bloke,
I love him like the day is long and he's so honest. Too honest,
maybe. But I was shitting myself when I played with him on
The White Room, bricking it. Still, must've been as bad for him as
it was for me. It was probably an honour for him to play one of
my songs for a start, let alone do it on TV.**" NOEL (1995)**

**"What was really scary was a session I had with him (Paul Weller),
Liam and Messrs Cradock and Fowler from Ocean Colour Scene.
Apart from anything else, they're completely fascist about their
musical taste. Liam'd say he liked such-and-such band and
Weller'd go, "Yeah, but look at the fucking shoes they're
wearing." Our kid's big thing at the moment is that The Strokes
are crap "cos their singer's called Julian. Sure, it is a shit name,
but musically they're fucking spot-on."** NOEL (2001)

"I don't hang around with anyone who isn't in the band - apart from
Weller, but he's almost an honorary member of our band anyway.**"**

NOEL (2001)

On Other Groups

"Don't talk to me about Nirvana. He was a sad man who couldn't handle the fame. We're stronger than that. And you can fuck your fucking Pearl Jam." LIAM (1994)

"Until six months ago, I thought Blondie were French." NOEL (1994)

"The thing about Bernard Butler leaving Suede is that the only person who could replace him is me. And I've got far better things to do." NOEL (1994)

"These bands that claim to be punk rock, they've just totally missed the point. They're all going on about The Clash and slogans and taking speed and all that, but they're all dead uptight about it. For me, punk rock was The Sex Pistols, and they were Big Time Fun. They covered The Small Faces and Chuck Berry and Johnny Rotten went on *Desert Island Discs* in 1977 and all he played was Neil Young..." NOEL (1994)

"It was me birthday the other day and I was walking up the street and I bump into fucking Morrissey! And I'm thinking, 'I've slagged him off in the past and he's going to fill me in here!' He's about six foot, fucking enormous and I'm only a skinny drug addict and he's going to kung-fu kick me in the chest! I thought he was going to batter me! So we walk past each other and sort of go '... All right? All right?'
"Then he notices I've got this huge bag of booze and he goes, 'Are you having a party?' And I go 'Yeah it's my birthday' and I was thinking to myself, 'Oh God, I can feel myself inviting him to my party, oh no!' It would've freaked me mates out if he'd turned up... Next thing this card appears through the letterbox from Morrissey saying, 'Sorry, I can't make it, but give us a ring if you want to go shoplifting.'" NOEL (1995)

HEROES & **INFLUENCES**

"Suggs is sad. He's ruined a top tune ('I'm Only Sleeping'). This is some Nineties 'I've got no money, so I'll stick out a bullshit version'. I should have done this song, not him. I'd sing it the same kind of way Lennon did... with feeling, only fresher for today." **LIAM (1995)**

THE SMITHS

"It's not good to see the likes of Shed Seven in the charts. They're a shit little band, and they've had too much press. They're just a crap version of The Smiths, and that singer sounds like Björk. He's an idiot. It's like, 'Oh, all right, another crap indie band'. What's the point?" LIAM (1995)

"Blur are a great pop band. 'Girls And Boys' was a good pop song, y'know? But they're not as good as us. Last year they were band of the year, but it should've been us. All our singles charted, we had sell-out tours, we were top of the album charts. We should've been band of the year." **LIAM (1995)**

"U2 write great songs. It's as simple as that, regardless of if Bono wants to save the fucking whale or the goldfish. I was out at a party the other night in London and he was there and I met him for the first time and he knows he's talked a lot of bullshit down the years but what a great guy! He sat down beside me and he sang me 'Slide Away' from the start to finish! Now for him to even have heard of Oasis let alone heard 'Slide Away', which wasn't even a single, is phenomenal enough. But for him to know all the fucking words..." NOEL (1995)

"After I heard Happy Mondays I actually didn't think there was another original band or an original form left in music until I heard the Portishead album. I wouldn't even know how to describe it. All I know is that it's fucking great." **NOEL (1995)**

"I went to my doctor and said, 'Can I get some Prozac?' And he went, 'No, fuck off.'"

"I've always sung me cock off, y'know, round my gaff. I'm double loud now. My style is banging it out."

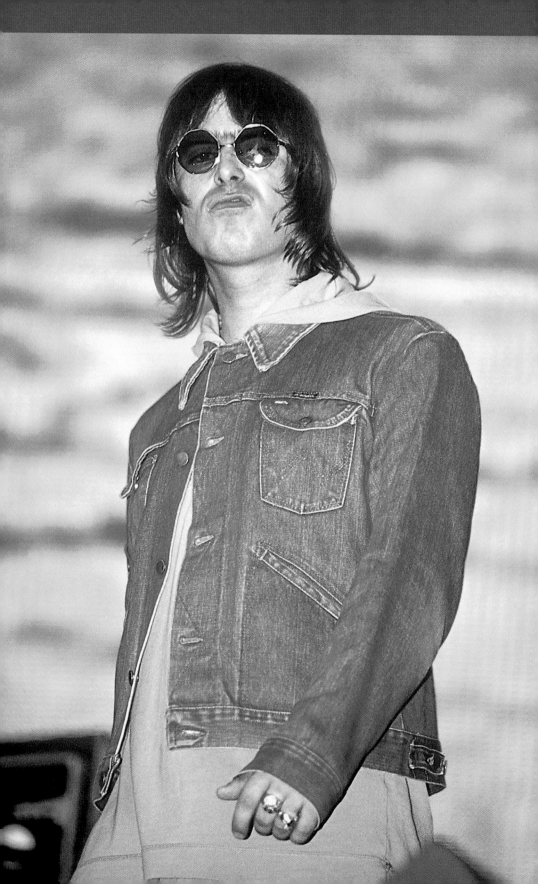

"Famous or not famous, I don't give a shit. Some famous people can be complete wankers."

> "Progression is going forwards. Going backwards is regression. Going sideways is just aggression."

“Bowie's the top, right? Written some of the greatest songs in rock and roll. He's always had good partners to work with – people like Mick Ronson and Brian Eno and all the rest.” NOEL (1995)

“Would we play with Bowie? Well, 20 years ago maybe but not now. He's just an old git.” NOEL (1995)

DAVID BOWIE

HAPPY MONDAYS

“Black Grape, fucking great! I was sat there with my hand over my mouth, the music's so fucking out there. Them and Pulp, I mean Pulp were brilliant. That 'Common People' should've been a Number 1 any week! The lyrics are hilarious, I think (Jarvis) is a top guy.” NOEL (1995)

“Evan Dando invited himself on tour with us. I didn't think I'd like him. I thought he'd be a bit of a knobhead, but he was really down to earth. The thing I like about Evan is he's not that deep, he talks shit and it's as funny as fuck and he's got total spirit. He'd turn up and, all of a sudden, everyone would be in a good mood. We'd all be sat there miserable as fuck and he'd burst in like some puppy dog and tell us to stop fighting.” NOEL (1995)

HEROES & **INFLUENCES** 99

"The Verve are a better band than we are. And Primal Scream, Cast, Ocean Colour Scene. All right, what I mean is they're as good as we are, not better. But they've not got involved in media bullshit bollocks like our so-called rivalry with Blur. They haven't been dragged into this 'Who's bigger? Who's better?' thing. But if it comes down to it, we are the biggest band in the country."

NOEL (1996)

"I'm a fan of records, not bands. There's even stuff The Beatles did I wouldn't bother replacing if they were robbed off me. (Radiohead's) *The Bends* is a great record, but *OK Computer* and *Amnesiac*... I really don't see what all the fuss is about. There's nothing on 'em that wasn't being done by Faust 25 years ago. As for the real 'Greatest Album Of All Time', it's got to be *Never Mind The Bollocks* by The Sex Pistols. Partly because it sounds like nothing else, and partly because they split up immediately afterwards. The records we listened to non-stop when we were making *Definitely Maybe*, and used as our benchmark, were *Never Mind The Bollocks* and The Who's *Live At Leeds*. Anything that lacked their intensity was thrown in the bin." **NOEL (2001)**

"The Strokes have got the tunes. They've got that thing and I don't know why, the un-nameable thing." NOEL (2001)

❝I think Suede and Blur suffered from the same thing – their singers became egomaniacs. Brett Anderson wanted Bernard Butler out and Damon Albarn is now running away with his band.**❞** **NOEL (2004)**

❝I just find The Darkness really, really inoffensive. It doesn't do anything for me.❞ NOEL (2004)

❝Cat Deeley bands – that's what The Flaming Lips and The Darkness are. But nothing against Cat Deeley, I'm sure she's a very nice girl.**❞** **LIAM (2004)**

❝(Coldplay's) Chris Martin can write a fucking song. I don't know what the fuck he's doing writing songs for Embrace, but he can write a song.❞ NOEL (2005)

❝The Subways? Any band that's got a bird in a miniskirt playing the bass is alright by me.**❞ NOEL (2005)**

❝The Zutons stepped in when Babyshambles couldn't be arsed turning up (at Southampton Rose Bowl) and they played one of the best sets I've ever seen in my life.❞ NOEL (2005)

❝Usually I don't condone this kind of music, but Jet've become our new best friends and I warmed to them after being on the road with them. I think they're great.**❞ NOEL (2005)**

THE ZUTONS

❝The Stands are Liverpool's best-kept secret.❞ NOEL (2005)

❝To me, The Coral are without doubt the best band in England, full stop. Their new record (*She Sings The Mourning*) has six absolute fucking genius songs on it.❞ NOEL 2005

❝**The Futureheads are quite simply the fucking weirdest band in Britain. I've no idea what their music is about, or what it means, but I fucking like it.**❞ NOEL 2005

❝Fucking amazing. Secret Machines have got the ghost of John Bonham playing drums.❞ **NOEL (2005)**

SECRET MACHINES

❝**If him (Nick Armstrong) and his group (The Thieves) can fucking sort their haircuts out, they'll be one of the biggest bands in Britain. They're pretty special, man. Like Cavern and Star Club-era Beatles played by Goths.**❞ NOEL (2005)

❝I just want to know what were those fuckers hoping to achieve out of this (*Pop Idol*)? What was that twat Dr Fox and those other cunts doing? Did they really think they'd find the new Elvis? They've

HEROES & **INFLUENCES** ❞

made a mockery of singing, of selling a million records. Will Young's in the *Guinness Book Of Records* for fuck's sake! But so what? So is a bloke who jumps off the Eiffel Tower and lands in a fucking tea cup. Did he write 'Strawberry Fields Forever?' No, so fuck off.**" NOEL (2002)**

"Radiohead don't want anyone else involved in that little thing they've got going on. Their thing is: Don't look at us. Don't photo us. Don't interview us. In fact, don't listen to our music. Where does it end? It ends with Thom Yorke saying 'I've written the most fantastic piece of classical music ever but the only way you can hear it is by jamming a jack plug into my ear'." NOEL (2002)

THE DARKNESS

"I believe in a thing called... er shit? I can't stand The Darkness' fucking fans either, they can fuck off.**" NOEL (2004)**

"Now I love The fucking Strokes, I love the way they look, I love what they stand for, I love the fucking drummer... but that second album? It's dog's piss." NOEL (2004)

" They're (Radiohead) a band of Morris dancers. **"**

LIAM (2002)

"That Gorillaz album – fucking rubbish." LIAM (2002)

" Black Rebel Motorcycle Club and The Vines are top live but the music's shit. **"** NOEL (2004)

"Alex Kapranos (Franz Ferdinand) reminds me of fucking Right Said Fred. You put on 'I'm Too Sexy For My Fucking Thing' next to their records and I bet you any money it's the same person. It's the same fucking person! He's just gone on the Atkins diet and grown his hair! Not my thing at all. I don't like quirky, weird music. It's not my cup of tea all that nonsense, million miles an hour music that's not going anywhere." LIAM (2005)

" I was a bit pissed so I went up to him (Bono) and said, 'You've made £150 million this year, but you still believe in God. How's that?' He said he wouldn't explain, but he gave me a couple of books. And it boils down to you either believe or you don't. And I don't believe there's a God who says, 'If you drink, do drugs and swear and rob houses you're not sitting on my cloud.' It's all cock. It's all fanny. The amount of times I've gone out in me back garden and shouted up to the sky, 'Come on then, fucking show me! Give me a sign!' **"** NOEL (2002)

"If that's what they (Scissor Sisters) call entertaining then let them 'ave it – bright colours and fucking weirdoes on stilts? I'm more entertaining than that cunt. And I'll rip his fucking vocal chords out any day because he's fucking rubbish." LIAM (2005)

" It's Charlotte Church for me, man. She could be the next Liam. She's got a great voice and she's fucking hammered and she freaks people out. **"** LIAM (2005)

HEROES & **INFLUENCES**

Noel & Liam
V Pete Doherty

PETE DOHERTY AND KATE MOSS

❝I'm not into smackheads. Smackheads need slaps. So what does the word Libertine mean? What does it mean? Freedom? He's fucking in the corner doing smack with a helmet on his head! There's nothing free about that. It's nasty, innit? If the kids like them, fair enough, but they're nowhere near like us. The music's rubbish for a start.❞

LIAM (2005)

❝I think two years ago, if you thought Pete Doherty, he was kind of untouchable. Now when you think of that guy who's always in the background of that picture with Kate Moss.**❞**

NOEL (2005)

❝I'm not sure he's (Pete Doherty) having a great time but, y'know, are you gonna be remembered as Kate Moss's boyfriend or a fucking artist?❞ NOEL (2005)

❝In six months he's (Pete Doherty) not put a record out, it's gonna smack of the emperor's new clothes, all of it. My opinion of him hasn't changed. His heart's in the right place but the people he's around are not that good for him.**❞ NOEL (2005)**

"I was disappointed (about his no-show supporting Oasis in Southampton) because I convinced Liam to get Babyshambles on because I'd seen them at Brixton and thought it was amazing. And Liam was going 'No man, I'm not having any of this shit,' and I was going, 'Fucking trust me man, it's great.'" NOEL (2005)

"We weren't furious, it was like, 'Oh, he's got to do a fashion show,' and it was like, 'Well, if fashion shows mean more of you, good luck to you.' He should change his name really, I think he's living up to his name as Babyshambles..." NOEL (2005)

"Pete Doherty wouldn't last a fucking rehearsal in Oasis. You'd be injecting washing-up liquid into you sphincter within half a fucking hour." NOEL (2005)

"It's not a question of professionalism. It's much more simple than that. This is the greatest group in the world and what we're not going to do is let anyone fuck it up." LIAM (2005)

"It's good to see Pete Doherty turned up – one big cock."
LIAM SPOTTING AN INFLATABLE FOUR FOOT PENIS AT THE V FESTIVAL (2005)

NOEL & LIAM V PETE DOHERTY

Look Back In Anger...
Oasis v Blur

❝I don't like what they're doing musically but they're all right. They're mad for it and I like them for that. It's only the press who keep going on about how we're supposed to be rivals, anyway.❞

LIAM (1995)

❝The guitarist I've got a lot of time for. The drummer I've never met – hear he's a nice guy. The bass player and the singer – I hope the pair of them catch AIDS and die because I fucking hate them two.❞ NOEL (1995)

❝I wish I'd never said some of the things I've said. That's done me no end of harm. I said what I said, and as soon as I said it I was (head in hands). I apologised in the next breath to the interviewer. Weeks later when I saw it I put the paper down and I said to Meg, 'I think I've blown it'. She read it and went, 'You idiot!' The first person on the phone was me mam saying, 'I didn't raise you to say things like that!'❞

NOEL ON THE 'DIE OF AIDS'
FIASCO (1996)

"The whole AIDS thing was my fault. She (journalist Miranda Sawyer) didn't ask any loaded questions but she did keep going on about Damon from Blur until I said I hated him. She said, 'How much?' and I said what I said. I've said worse things about people. It just hasn't gotten written up." NOEL (1997)

"I wanted me five Number 1s in a row, didn't I, 'cos the Jam had four... but that's just me. I was more pissed off about the way it happened. It was their decision (to release singles on the same day) and we knew that all along. It seems now they were basically lying. Very childish.

"We've never done anything untoward to any band apart from slag them off. We've never tried to scupper or pull the rug out from under any band's career. I would love for Pulp to go in at Number 1 one week, then the next week us, then the next week Blur, then whoever else the week after. You don't want to be competing against each other 'cos that gets you fucking nowhere." NOEL (1995)

PULP

"Your band's shite, and I've got the arse and the bollocks to say so to your face." LIAM TO DAMON AT THE BRAT AWARDS (1995)

"I was double rude to Justine (Frischmann, Elastica) the other night, going, 'Go and get your tits out'. It's her boyfriend (Damon Albarn, Blur), innit, 'cos I love getting at him 'cos he's a dick. If anyone said that to my bird I'd chin him. But I fancy her big time! I'm having her, man. In the next six months it'll be all over the press – I'll have been with her. Don't say that though, 'cos I'm mad for her and that'd screw it right up..." LIAM (1995)

"It's the press that created that whole thing. Did it get annoying? Of course it did. I remember being down the King's Road the day that Chelsea played Man United and I went into this pub that turned out to be a Chelsea local. Someone saw I was there and they put 'Parklife' on the jukebox, like, nine times." NOEL (1995)

"I really don't think Blur and us would have gone into the charts at 1 and 2 if it hadn't been for the press building it up into such a big battle. It sells issues, doesn't it?" NOEL (1995)

"We lost the battle, won the war. I always said we would. It's not a quick sprint. We know how good we are, there are people who love our band, we know how good they think we are. We don't have to prove ourselves to anyone, least of all journalists."

NOEL (1996)

"The Blur/Oasis thing was very silly but it was fun. I meant every word I said. They're still a bunch of goons, but…" LIAM (2002)

"The thing that still pisses me off to this day is that cuntfuck said we engineered the battle with his bunch of wankers. Oasis don't need to compete with a bunch of cunts who did A-level music. They're fakers." NOEL (2002)

LIAM WITH DAMON ALBARN FROM BLUR

OASIS V **BLUR**

Rock The Vote... Oasis Play Politics

❝I see things for what they are. I don't look into things deeply. Y'know, you wake up, you do what you do, then you go to bed. Nothing changes. That's why at this moment, to all intents and purposes, we're the biggest band in England. The kids have just gone, 'These guys know what's what.'**❞** NOEL (1994)

❝I don't wear that for nothing (a crucifix on chain). I don't know what it symbolises, but I believe in a higher power. I don't believe that on Monday morning some white-bearded geezer with fuckin' nothing better to do created the planets. Bollocks to that!❞

NOEL (1996)

❝When people of my generation left school, they had only three choices offered them: football, music or the dole. That's why there are so many big rock groups from the North.**❞** NOEL (1996)

"The notion of a work ethic no longer exists in Manchester, because we don't like to work. Myself, I had the chance to do work which pleases me: I went into a studio, recorded a song, released a record, I have a good life. What's more, I bring some pleasure to others. Most of my mates hate their work." NOEL (1996)

"In the Sixties, when you heard of a family friend out of work, you knew it was temporary. Today, you start off life sure you'll never find a job. So you adapt your lifestyle to this new fact." **NOEL (1996)**

"I hate the way anyone from the working class who makes money, the working class turns on them. The people in my band, we'll be working class till we die. We were brought up socialists and we'll die socialists." NOEL (1996)

OASIS PLAY POLITICS

NOEL MEETS TONY BLAIR, WITH ALAN McGEE, AT 10 DOWNING STREET

❝I had a ticket for the Labour Party party, but I had that much fun watching Portillo and the others done over I stayed home in front of the TV. It was all champagne, brandy and cigars round our house.❞ NOEL (1997)

❝All that Tony Blair stuff's been blown out of proportion. People were asking me who I was going to vote for, I'd tell 'em Labour and give them a reason. Then all of a sudden I'm being portrayed as the new spokesman for New Labour, which is ridiculous. There's no way I got Tony Blair elected. The people of England elected him. I mean, I voted for him because I'm working class. It was good to see the working class getting mobilised and off their arses and down to the polling booths and actually voting the Tories out. But I don't think it had anything to do with me.❞

NOEL (1997)

❝Inevitably, they will make a fucking balls of it. Do they know where Bin Laden is? What happens if he ends up in China? Are they going to send the SEALS and the Marines into Belfast to take out the IRA and the Loyalists?❞

NOEL (2001) ON THE WAR AGAINST TERRORISM

"Walking through the doors at 10 Downing Street, not as a plumber but an invited guest. I'm glad I did it to have a look, but in terms of New Labour, I recognise now that we were conned. We thought Blair was John F Kennedy, when in fact he was John Major with a better PR team!" NOEL (2001)

"Robin Cook was a principled politician who resigned because he was against the Iraq war. The band respect him for that."

NOEL (2005)

"Correct me if I am wrong, but are they hoping that one of these guys from the G8 is going to see Annie Lennox singing 'Sweet Dreams' and think 'Fuck me, she might have a point there.' Or Keane doing 'Somewhere Only We Know' and some Japanese businessman looks at him and says 'We should really drop that debt, you know.' It isn't going to happen is it?" NOEL (2005)

"You get people saying Live8's the greatest thing that's ever been organised in Europe, and you're thinking 'Er... D-Day?'"

NOEL (2005)

ANNIE LENNOX

OASIS PLAY POLITICS

Cast No Shadow...
Songwriting

❝But if it all ended tomorrow, I'd still write songs because that's what I do. I did it when I was broke and on the dole and, ever since I was 11, playing the guitar has been my only escape.❞ NOEL (1994)

❝Noel won't let me (write), but I can't really yet anyway. Elvis never wrote a fuckin' song in his life. Say, in the future if I started learning and writing top tunes, I still don't think he'd be up for it... I know for a fact, even if he was going dry, he wouldn't play my songs, him. Never. I'm not very happy with that, but that's the way it is innit?❞ LIAM (1994)

❝I've been writing songs for 13 years... I haven't always been this good. I started off pretty bad, then got to pretty average, and now at this stage I consider myself being all right, better than 90 percent... No, better than everybody else bar Paul Weller and... Paul Weller, really!❞ NOEL (1994)

❝I sometimes think people have got the wrong end of us, that life's a bowl of cherries and we're just like the cherry pickers. There is barely time to wipe the shit from your

shoes – which is another one of my fine lyrics, I might add. It's hard writing upbeat songs when you're really working hard and you're away from home all the time and you're... pissed!**"** NOEL (1995)

" I'm not always comfortable writing really personal songs, it's never been what we're about. When I hear Eddie Vedder going on about being abused as a child, I just think, 'Fuck off, don't tell me about it, I don't want to hear it.' 'Talk Tonight' and 'Slide Away' have made me realise I can write personal songs, but it's not like that's what they're all going to be. We can do really good straightforward pop as well.**"** NOEL (1995)

" I hate writing lyrics. Don't like it at all. It's a problem. When we came up to the studio I had all these songs written and they were all arranged, they all had melodies but I just found myself repeating myself over the things I wrote on *Definitely Maybe*. It's becoming a pain in the fucking arse, so, if there's anybody out there who's got some lyrics they don't want, give them to me."

NOEL (1995)

" All the stuff on *Definitely Maybe* was written when we didn't have a record deal and I wasn't writing with anything in mind. But now when I write something I think of what all the people in brackets are going to read into it... we're not as happy-go-lucky as we used to be.**"** NOEL (1995)

" I don't ever want to bare my soul. Lyrics to me are an ongoing grey area and I don't know what it's about. I'm a happy-go-lucky character. I'm not that miserable. But I can never ever let anyone into my world." NOEL (1996)

" Every songwriter is afraid of picking the guitar up and nothing coming out. That's why we keep going. Look at Lee Mavers (of the La's), he got writer's block. That's why I'm going to record four albums before I lose the point, unlike Lee, who only did one. And The Stone Roses didn't do anything for five years.**"** NOEL (1996)

SONGWRITING

" Me, if I didn't have football and the guitar, God knows what I would have become. I got the talent to write songs and live from it. So I do my best to amuse people. Because I know that's all I can do for them. Three and a half minutes of happiness in a gloomy and banal life, I'm afraid that's my only contribution. " NOEL (1996)

" As long as I believe I have something valid to put out as a piece of music then I'll keep doing it. As soon as I feel it's not, I'll stop and do something else like open a chippy or work in a butcher's shop. **"** NOEL (1996)

" I'm not Morrissey. I'm not Bob Dylan. I'm not Brett Anderson. They are better lyricists than I'll ever be. " NOEL (1996)

" People always say, 'Don't you want to be innovative?' Well, no. We just want to make good records. People are afraid of the obvious. We always go for the obvious. People want to hear a song, then hum it, then wind it back again and again. **"** NOEL (1996)

" When I'm writing a song, that's it. I'll sit up in this chair 48 hours, smoking, drinking, playing the same line over again. I put that girl through hell. When I'm going through all that, them chaps are in their cosy beds, with their cosy lives – it's all cosy for them. And when it's time to make a new album, they wake up in the morning and go, 'Where's the songs?' It's me who has to come up with them. " NOEL (1996)

" I'm not the songwriter. I'm just the fookin' singer. **"** LIAM (1997)

" I write the songs for this group. Always have and always will do. " NOEL (1997)

" If you let Liam write a song, then Bonehead's got to write a song, then Guigsy's got to write some songs, then Alan... and it's no longer Oasis. Oasis is my songs - and it's as simple as that. **"**

NOEL (1997)

"I've written three songs, but no-one's gonna hear 'em. Maybe in the future people can hear 'em. But I'm not gonna sell 'em to a record company 'cos they'd only destroy 'em. I prefer to keep things personal. It's got to be a personal vibe 'cos everything else is out in the open. Everyone knows what kind of underpants I wear, what kind of socks I wear, how many times I pick my nose in a day - so fuck 'em all, I'm gonna just keep these songs to myself.**"** LIAM (1997)

"I've been writing songs, seriously, since I was 14. Some songs take five, ten, fifteen minutes to write. Others take three weeks. I suppose they come from somewhere between your soul and your stomach. I wouldn't like to know, because it surprises me when I write something these days.**"** NOEL (1997)

"I'm bored and can't be bothered writing music any more. The bigger the monster becomes, the harder it is to manoeuvre. I've started thinking that maybe it's time to scale it down - y'know, shed some of the weight or perhaps try new things altogether. To be honest, I don't know if I can be arsed putting out another rock'n'roll record. I deserve a fucking break.**"**

NOEL (2001)

SONGWRITING **"**

" They (songs on the new album) all sound quite similar to be honest. The thing with Gem and Andy is they were fans of the band anyway, so it was like, 'Look you're not writing for Hurricane #1 (Andy's old band) and you're not writing for Heavy Stereo (Gem's old band). You know the drill, y'know what I mean?' With Liam, I taught him how to write songs anyway, so he's gonna write in that style. **"** NOEL (2001)

" The optimistic songs are very optimistic and the angry ones are very angry, that's just the way I've been feeling lately. There is no middle ground for me no more, for a couple of years everything was all right. Now it's really good or its fuckin' shit. But I'm glad to get back to my extreme behaviour rather than walking around with a glass of champagne going, 'Isn't life great?'" NOEL (2001)

" I never ever sat down and said, 'Right, I'm going to write a song about getting divorced', or what it's like to be estranged from my child. I just think it's pathetic. Eric Clapton writing songs about his dead son? That's exploiting the fact that your child is dead. You're making money out of it, man. Morally that's wrong. **"** NOEL (2001)

" I wouldn't be so calculating as to write about my own pain. You would have to be some wanker if you went through life and weren't affected by anything that happened to you. Let me tell you, when you people dissect the lyrics for this album you can read anything into anything. I could recite the lyrics for 'I Am The Walrus' and convince you it's about me and me alone. " NOEL (2001)

" They're just good songs - as good as fucking magic, they're as good as John Lennon. The vocals are the best I've done ever. Andy Bell's playing drums, Gem's on bass, Johnny Marr's playing guitar and it's really good. Andy'll do his song, Gem'll do his song and we'll just keep writing and writing until we're ready to record. We don't know when we're gonna put another album out, but we're gonna keep writing- there are four songwriters in Oasis now instead of one, and all four of them are good. **"** LIAM (2001)

"There's one called 'Song Bird' which is better than anything on fucking *Revolver*. They're not pop music. There's probably one pop song - just two chords all the way through, the melody's great. The rest are proper dark, weird shit. People will probably hate them. But it's better than anything Radiohead are doing."

LIAM (2001)

"Liam says he's written some songs that are better than the ones on The Beatles' *Revolver*. It's bullshit. Nobody is capable of writing anything better than the songs on *Revolver*. The songs that Liam's written are all right. Maybe they're better than the songs that I was writing when I was his age. He's not as good as John Lennon. He's not even as good as Jack Lemmon, God bless him. He's written a few pretty good songs for the last record. But nothing more and nothing less than that. He's not in John Lennon's class. Only I am capable of that." NOEL (2000)

"It's been difficult lately, because I don't want to write songs about the break-up of my marriage. Oasis don't do angst, we're more an anthemic, celebratory group. So I don't know really what I want to write at the moment. But I've got three new songs: 'Revival', which is a bit like 'Louie Louie' but a bit more Sex Pistols. Then there's one called 'Shout It Out Loud', which is your basic Neil Young meets Pink Floyd meets Oasis, a bit of an anthem, a bit of a flag-waver. And then there's one called 'She Is Love', which is probably a bit like The Monkees or The Byrds. They're just songs I've written, they're not the blueprints for an album or anything." NOEL (2001)

“As long as there are some of my songs on the album, I’ll be happy. Mind you, I wouldn’t want to be the producer refereeing that.” NOEL (2001)

“I don’t want Ronan Keating singing one of my songs. I’d rather set fire to myself.” NOEL (2002)

“I’m now 36 but when you’re 21 and you’re single and you haven’t got any baggage you can just sit and write songs all night, where as now I’ve got kids and this and that, I don’t have the time to write as much as I used to. I was talking to Weller about this and his next album will be his 640th album or something, and what more is there to fucking say? It’s just a constant struggle to say the same thing differently.” NOEL (2004)

“I’ll be the best songwriter in the fucking world, never mind the country.” LIAM (2002)

“He’s (Liam) at the stage I was at 20, where you’re writing song after song after song.” NOEL (2005)

“I suppose I’m going to have a musical nosebleed soon. I can’t keep it (emotions) locked up for ever. I know it’s got to come out somewhere. I just don’t know if I’m looking forward to it.” NOEL (2002)

ANDY BELL

SONGWRITING

The Records

Definitely Maybe

❝This is the third time we've recorded it. After the first time, I have to admit that I lied about it. I said it was the greatest album of the last five years when I know deep in my heart that it wasn't. But it is now, and I'm fuckin' not lying. It's 11 singles – well, ten singles and a really nice, corny track at the end. All I ask is that people don't try to analyse the songs.❞ NOEL (1994)

❝I think the sound of *Definitely Maybe* was a bit one-dimensional, everything was the same tone, whack it up to ten and off we go.❞

NOEL (1995)

❝Recording an album should never have been this difficult. I was busy telling everyone it was the greatest record ever made but it was sounding like shit.❞ NOEL (1994)

❝I knew the first mix wasn't right, but I was that fed up with it all I'd begun not to care. I know that a song never comes out on tape the way it sounds in your head, but these mixes were so wide of the mark it was a fucking joke. The demos were better.❞

NOEL (1994)

❝I think *Definitely Maybe* will always be seen as one of the greatest ever début albums, but I always knew we could be even better.❞

NOEL (1995)

❝People said to me after 'Live Forever', 'Where are you gonna go after that?' And I was like, I don't think it's that good. I think it's a fucking good song but I think I can do better.❞ NOEL (1995)

(What's The Story) Morning Glory

"No one ever makes good second albums. They're usually just full of the fillers that wouldn't fit on the first one. We're going to be the exception. Originally, I wanted to call it *Flash In The Pan*, but now I think it might be called *Morning Glory*." NOEL (1995)

"The music is basically the same. It's Oasis. But this time we will have a lot more money to play with, so we can do what the fuck we want. People at the record company now recognise us as a big band, so we can say, 'We want a string quartet, but we don't just want one, we want two of them'. And they go, 'All right, fine'. I reckon it'll be the same but a bit more diverse-sounding. It's the lyrics that'll change." NOEL (1994)

"Because it was written when we were on the dole, *Definitely Maybe*, was about dreaming about being a rock'n'roll star. And this is an album about what it's like to be in a group – which six days out of seven is a laugh, but half the songs on this album were written on the seventh day. People are saying it's not as immediate as the last one. I don't care. I know people are gonna get this album, because I put a lot of faith in people's ears.
"There's no such thing as a perfect album. There never will be. You should never write that perfect song, 'cos if you do you might as well pack it all in. I remember Bob Mould once said you're always looking for that song, and if you ever write that song then where else is there to go? Same as me." NOEL (1995)

"All we can do is make the records. If people don't like it, then fine. And I'm sure we'll lose fans who were expecting another *Definitely Maybe*, but I hope we gain as many who'll hear *Morning Glory* and think, 'I never expected to hear that from this band'. That's all you can do. If you think about it too deeply you become a fucking lunatic and blow your head off, like Kurt Cobain, who felt he owed millions of people around the world something – and he didn't." NOEL (1995)

THE RECORDS

"We'd put six tracks down. I was working 18 hours a day at the time in the studio and I came back one night and half of fucking Monmouth were in my fucking room. I'm well up for a bit of partying but all these people were there and I was 'Who are you and what are you doing in my studio?'

"I found the others and I said, 'We're here to make a record not National Lampoon's *Animal House*. I'm off to Jersey for a couple of weeks, go and sort yourselves out.' They freaked out, but I had to remind them that we were working." NOEL (1995)

"When the first reviews came out and they weren't negative but they weren't as positive as I thought they'd be some people in the band were flapping a bit. But I was like, 'Look, we all knew when we made that record how good it was.'" NOEL (1996)

"'Roll With It' is just a typical fuckin' Oasis thing. Shut up moaning and fuckin' get on with it. You've gotta say what you say, and be who you be. It's the same sentiments as there is in nearly every song we do. Is it about Liam? Is it fuck! They're just words that come out, none of them are about anything really. We just thought it was a good song for the summer." NOEL (1995)

"'Don't Look Back In Anger' reminds me of a cross between 'All The Young Dudes' and summat The Beatles might've done. The chorus goes, 'So Sally can wait...' But I don't actually know anybody called Sally. It was just a word that fitted, and I thought, Y'know, might as well throw a girl's name in there. It's gotta guarantee somebody a shag off a bird called Sally, hasn't it?" NOEL (1995)

"People have said to us that 'Champagne Supernova' is our message to the Stone Roses, but that's thinking too deep. It's about anyone, y'know... It doesn't necessarily mean getting high, but getting older, having a good time..." NOEL (1995)

THE RECORDS

Be Here Now

"The new songs sound like a 28-year-old man living in England who has been in a rock band for four years. It's not cynical, just observations on life. *Definitely Maybe* was bombastic, just us screaming we want to be in a rock'n'roll band. *Morning Glory* is me observing my immediate life. The new stuff is more worldly."

NOEL (1996)

"*Morning Glory* was written on an acoustic guitar, it shows in the likes of 'Wonderwall' and 'Don't Look Back In Anger'. But now I've got me amp set up at home and started writing on electric guitar, the new stuff is sort of a cross between the two albums. There's harmonies in it and obviously it's really, really melodic." **NOEL (1996)**

"I didn't set out consciously to write a long record or a batch of long songs. That's just the way it came out. Some of the songs could be better. There are three or four old ones - the rest are quite recent. I've been listening to the songs for so long now that I'm getting a bit bored with it." NOEL (1997)

"*Be Here Now* has shockingly bad lyrics. But I will say in my own demonic, drug-induced state I wrote an album in 14 days and - count them - that sold seven-and-a-half million copies. If I'd actually tried at that point in my life I'd have been fucking God. As it was I was more interested in having a party, so it was like, well, I'll spend half an hour fucking about with this and then we'll be off down the beach." **NOEL (2001)**

"You should've tried *Be Here Now* on nine grams of Charlie 'cos that's what it was written on. Well, everybody has a shit period and hopefully we've had ours. And this new album... is fuckin' mega! I'm not a fuckin' drug addict any more. So it's not just 'Well, fuck it, that'll do', which is what *Be Here Now* should have been called." NOEL (2001)

"I've got a song called 'All Around The World', which I've always said could win the Eurovision Song Contest. Maybe we'll enter next year, just for the fuck of it." NOEL (1995)

"I hadn't believed this journalist a couple of years ago when he told me that *Be Here Now* is one of Marilyn Manson's favourite records, but, yeah, it's true." NOEL (2001)

Standing On The Shoulder Of Giants (album)

"It's the only album I've written while I was straight. And it was recorded while everyone was sober. I suppose in that sense it's a bit of a first for us. As for being a mature, adult record, I don't really know what that means. You become very emotionally stunted when you're on drugs, particularly on coke. With the last bunch of albums when I would eventually come to write the lyrics, I would write any old shit that rhymed really." NOEL (2000)

"I don't think people think it's a bad album, it's just not this earth-shattering experience. But is any band that important after five albums?" NOEL (2000)

"The lyrics on 'I Can See A Liar' were fucking shit, but I knew that in the first place and for the life of me I couldn't come up with anything better. I should have written another verse for 'Put Yer Money Where Your Mouth Is', but other than that I would stand by all the fucking songs on that record. It's not very 'single-heavy', which is also probably true of *Be Here Now*." NOEL (2001)

THE RECORDS

"When (Creation boss Alan) McGee first heard 'Where Did It All Go Wrong?', he said, 'Fucking hell, that's the first time I've ever heard you pissed off in a song.' I wanted to change my life. I was still living in London. I was getting frustrated. I'd made this big decision in my life to kick the drugs and there were all these people saying, 'Come on! Have a line, it's rock'n'roll!' They wouldn't know rock'n'roll if it bit them in the arse! I thought, 'How did I end up in a room with all these twats?' I wanted to get my head straight." NOEL (2000)

"People say it was shite and people say it was good, I think it's a great album. I think it's a great fourth album, and if that's not good enough then fine. People say it's amazing, it's not amazing, nothing's amazing, y'know what I mean? I think it's great, otherwise it wouldn't have come out. Just because you get a couple of bad reviews doesn't mean I'm going to go, 'Oh, you're right'. I stand by everything we do, because we put it out and we are happy with it at the time." LIAM (2001)

"'Go Let It Out' started out as this slow Beta Band thing, then it speeded up and became a psychedelic pop song. It was something out of nothing. I tend to write songs in threes, and when I played the first two new songs - they're B-sides now - to my manager and Liam they said, 'Hmm, they're all right, I suppose.' But when that one came on, Liam sat up on the sofa, held up his bottle of Jack Daniels and said, 'Yes! It's good to be back!'" NOEL (2000)

"When you look back at it, it was a bit crazy. The producer (Owen Morris) was just as mad as us, you know what I mean, he was drinking as much as us. It was just we weren't concentrating on the job that we were doing. But the songs are fucking great. I don't particularly think my singing was good 'cos I was off it and that, but other than that, it was a fucking great album. You know, it's not a fucking shit album. It's the *Phantom Menace* of albums. Listen, it was the album we were out to do and that was the way it was done. I'm not saying it's the best, but it's definitely not the worst.

Maybe we didn't go any further, maybe we didn't take a step forward, but we didn't take a step back.

"And going down to the sales, it sold six million copies. People say it's poor sales... six million people fucking liked it, so what are you talking about?" LIAM (2000)

THE RECORDS

Heathen Chemistry

❝There's a Northern flat-cap anthem that we're going to finish off with a proper Salvation Army band.❞ NOEL (2001)

❝All the backing tracks are done and it's a fantastic album of instrumentals at the moment. Hand it over to the singer and it just slows down and becomes this one really long drawn-out, painful process. So to be honest with you I don't know when it'll come out now. It's down to him. Something will be out next year, but someone's gonna have to give him a fucking kick up the arse man. It's just laziness, that's all it is, and maybe a lack of confidence.❞

NOEL (2001)

❝We had it mixed and the artwork done and everything, I've still got the finished version in front of me now. I just thought it wasn't really good enough. We decided to go back to the drawing board. It was a good vibe, but it just needed more work. it was one verse and one chorus repeated over and over again, much in the same vein as 'Roll With It'. We got away with it in '95 but there's a lot of decent songwriters around now, know what I mean? To me, it would be just like, 'Is that it?'❞

NOEL (2001) ON THE FIRST SINGLE FOR THE NEW ALBUM

❝Even the slow songs are fuckin' loud. But I think what I meant by it being closer to *Definitely Maybe* was the spirit of it all and, up until three months ago, the spontaneity of it all. It was very much off-the-cuff, like, 'There's the amp, let's fuckin' have it!'. We didn't think about it much, until Liam's now gone away and thought about it for three months and is disappearing up his own arse, I think. But in its spirit it's more like *Definitely Maybe* because of the lyrical content.❞ NOEL (2001)

❝It's punk rock. And moody. And well done, proper - none of that weird fooking Radiohead bollocks, none of that indie fooking rubbish. It's the Pistols and the Beatles, man - it's us.❞ LIAM (2001)

66 'Song Bird', it's up an' it's roarin'.
'Better Man', that's pretty odd, and
'Born On A Different Cloud', which
is fooking rockin'. 99

**LIAM (2001) ON THE SONGS HE PENNED
FOR THE NEW ALBUM**

66 **We've been in the studio, I just
fucking wanted to put them down
- just to get them out. I went in
the studio the other week with
Johnny Marr, and Noel came down
one day and played drums. We
just fucked about and I just said,
'This is how I think we should
record these days. Do it in a
fucking week, instead of spending
a month in the pub and a month
arguing.' Everyone was like,
'Yeah, right, you wouldn't be able
to do that,' so I done it. Ten songs
in a week, all done, mixed, the
fucking lot, all ready to go. And
they're just my songs and they're
fucking classics.** 99 LIAM (2001)

66 It's exactly what you'd expect
from us - and that's not to sound
narrow-minded. A lot of bands
these days go out of their way
not to sound like themselves.
If anything we've gone the other
route. We're desperately trying
to sound like Oasis. This is us
- without experimentation. 99

NOEL (2001)

THE RECORDS 99

"I don't give a flying fuck if people think it's ('She Is Love') a soppy song. There's a skip button on your CD player if you don't like it." NOEL (2002)

ZAK STARKEY

"We experimented a little bit on the last album, but this time we wanted to come back to a rock'n'roll record." LIAM (2002)

"Apart from 'She Is Love' there's nothing on this album that's personal. I wouldn't want anyone to listen to this and flatter themselves that I've written a song about them. 'She Is Love' is about waking up on a sunny Sunday morning and the woman you love saying, 'Do you want a cup of tea?' That song is about being 30-odd years of age and thinking that life is good and my missus is cool. With here, there's no hassle. There's no, 'You have to be like *this* or where were you 'till 5am?' None of that fucking shit."

NOEL (2002)

"It's the first time I've ever gone, 'Right, I'm going to write a Number One single.' We'd recorded it ('The Hindu Times'), mixed it, mastered it, done the artwork and I got up on the day it was supposed to be announced and phoned everyone up and said, 'I don't like it'. Liam, like the woman he is, goes fucking apeshit. 'You're off your fucking head! You're smoking too much pot! I'm not going to speak to you, you fucking dick!' and slams the phone down. I thought, 'If I put that out now it's going to kill me for the rest of me fucking life. It's going to be the 'Be Here Now' syndrome, when I should have taken more time to write the lyrics.' That's why that record annoys me so much." **NOEL (2002)**

"'Force Of Nature' is supposed to be the first single. It started off with a sample from 'Nightclubbing' by Iggy Pop. I only sung it once. Liam went in there and sung it (them listened to my demo) and said, 'That's one of the best fucking vocals I've ever heard.' And I was like, 'Cool'." NOEL (2002)

"I don't like singing at all. I only started doing a couple of acoustic songs in the middle of the set to give Liam a break for his voice. In America it used to go down a fucking storm." **NOEL (2002)**

"A friend of mine was going through a pretty bad time with his kids and I sort of wrote it ('Stop Crying Your Heart Out') with him in mind." NOEL (2002)

"I thought 'Be Here Now' kicked arse and... *Morning Glory* was a bag of shite." **LIAM (2002)**

"*Morning Glory* was grossly over-rated and *Be Here Now* I find grossly offensive. I listened to it about six months ago and I had a pillow over my ears. I won't bullshit you, we'd fucked everything up by then and we blew it." NOEL (2002)

THE RECORDS

"I'm the singer and the only personal lyrics of his I'm singing is I've got a 12-inch cock, d'ya want some? I don't mind singing that. I've got to be able to put my own emotions into it or else I won't touch it." LIAM (2002)

"'Force Of Nature' was written for the film *Love, Honour & Obey*, for a scene where Jonny Lee Miller has nicked all the drugs. Check the date. 1998. I was happily married then." NOEL (2002)

Don't Believe The Truth

"I was saying to Richard Fearless, 'We don't really need anyone to freshen up the sound, we don't want anyone to produce it. The reason we want Death in Vegas to produce it is because we want you to, not because we need you to. I'm quite capable of doing it myself, I can happily make a psychedelic rock record of my own. But I can't be fucking arsed this time...' why should I do all the fucking work?" NOEL (2003)

"Those three weeks were like the ones we'd done *Definitely Maybe* in, but 10 years after. We were sat in a cloud of smoke going, 'Man, the planets are fucking aligning'. But when we went back to listen to what we'd got it was like, Oops, hang on a minute, that doesn't sound very good." NOEL (2005)

"'Turn Up The Sun' was written by Andy and it's always been the first track. A bit like Black Rebel Motorcycle Club. A stomper."
NOEL (2005)

"Imagine Bob Dylan singing (Velvet Underground's) 'Waiting For The Man' – with that kind of frantic drumbeat all the way through ('Mucky Fingers')." NOEL (2005)

"'Lyla' is our poppiest thing since 'Roll With It'. Annoyingly catchy and sounds a bit like The Who."
NOEL (2005)

"'Love Like A Bomb' is one of Liam's. It starts off acoustic and Martin Duffy from Primal Scream plays this kind of country piano solo, which brings it elsewhere." NOEL (2005)

" 'The Importance Of Being Idle' is a cross between being The Kinks and The La's, about being a lazy fucker. I spent a lot of last summer just sitting around the house doing nothing, really impressed by my lack of drive.**" NOEL (2005)**

"'Stop The Clocks' a song that's been around for a long, long time. But it might not make it. There's a bit of debate going on at the moment." NOEL (2005)

" 'Part Of The Queue' is one of mine with a weird 3/4 rhythm that's a bit Shack-doing-Love. The idea came to me standing in a queue in a fucking supermarket in the West End. All I wanted was a packet of Rizla.**" NOEL (2005)**

"'Keep The Dream Alive' is a song by Andy that sounds like The Stone Roses. You can imagine Reni playing drums and Ian waving his mic." NOEL (2005)

" 'Guess God Thinks I'm Abel' is a Liam tune that's kind of slowish and acoustic. The drums don't come in till the last 10 seconds and it finishes in a hail of feedback.**" NOEL (2005)**

"For about three months, we all thought the song was called 'Guess God Thinks I'm Able,' as in an able-bodied man, so we're coming to write the track listing one day and (Liam) goes, 'It's not fucking Able', and he wrote it out and we were all kinda looking at each other, going, 'Hmmm.' I had to go back and listen to it, and then I sat down thinking about it and the story of Cain and Abel." NOEL (2005)

THE RECORDS

"I'm thinking, 'Well that's very religious and biblical and it's a bit deep.' But… the first line of the song ('Guess God Thinks I'm Abel') is 'You could be my lover' which… you'd have to speak to Liam about. He has a religious fixation with (Abel) and Jesus, I think. It's very strange." NOEL (2005)

"Gem wrote 'A Bell Will Ring' and it's the closest anybody's ever got to sound like (The Beatles') *Revolver.* We did it live and it's kind of all one chord." NOEL (2005)

"It's taken me eight and a half years to write 'Let There Be Love'. We both sing, like the Self-Righteous Brothers. It's a fitting anthem to finish off the record." NOEL (2005)

"'The Meaning Of Soul' is like Elvis on crack. Zak's playing a box of Weetos with two wooden spoons. We played it at Glastonbury like The Stooges, but kept the Elvis '56 vibe for the record."
NOEL (2005)

Singles, Out-takes and Bonus Tracks

"Oasis B-sides aren't just throwaway fillers. I'm not going to waste my time sitting down writing second-rate songs. I don't think there's ever been a song we've put out that I'm ashamed of. You're not going to get twenty dance mixes of 'Wonderwall'. Sorry." NOEL (1995)

"I've always had complete confidence in what we could do. In the beginning there was a masterplan to the extent that I knew that 'Whatever', one of the first songs I wrote, would be a Christmas Top Five hit, but I think anyone who heard it could have told you that." NOEL (1995)

“When I wrote 'Talk Tonight' I suddenly realised, 'Hey, I can really write a personal song'. Because of all the things that were going on when it was written, it was always going to be very personal, but I don't know if I'll ever write anything as direct again. You can't just do something like that to order.” NOEL (1995)

“That Mike Flowers Pops lot are going to have a hit with 'Wonderwall'. I think it's a good version. They asked me to be in the video, but I couldn't do it. I hope it's a hit, though. Publishing, man!” **NOEL (1995)**

“'Acquiesce' took twenty minutes to write. I was on the train down here and I knew we needed another song. The train broke down and I wrote it then. I always write best when I'm under pressure or pissed off. It's better just writing in a burst than spend months going back and changing things. Most of the best things we've recorded have been done really quickly.” NOEL (1995)

“What I find... not upsetting, but annoying is, like, we've got a single out yesterday. Now, on Monday morning people'll start writing about how it failed to get to Number 1, or the Top 5. But nobody writes how Travis have failed to get to Number 1. ('Sunday Morning Call' entered the charts at Number 4.)”

NOEL (2000)

TRAVIS

THE RECORDS

"When I was younger I could sit in a room and knock off three songs a day, like 'Some Might Say' and 'Whatever' and a bunch of B-sides. But y'know, I'm not 26 any more. People think: Aw, give him two weeks and he'll write another album. It's not like that." NOEL (2000)

"I fucking loathe videos. This is not the reason why I started a band, to stand on a video stage all day and mime a song 500 times, knowing that when you get to the end of the 499th, you're thinking, 'I don't even fucking like this song any more, it's stupid'. But it's a necessary evil.**"** **NOEL (2005)**

"I turn up, they put their little cross (of tape) on the stage, and they say, 'You stand there and do your thing', and you do it as best you can and hope that the guy who's doing the video does a good job. There's only ever been one criterion, and that's to make us look 10 years younger. You get that right ('Lyla' video) and I'm fine." NOEL (2005)

"What the fuck do producers do anyway? Sit there, drink coffee and tell you how shit you are.**"** **LIAM (2003)**

"I've never met him (Ringo Starr). Because he lives in LA, we were hoping he might show his face. But he was in England when we were recording there, so it wasn't meant to be." NOEL (2005)

" *Morning Glory* cast such a shadow over us. That's gone now. We've got proper musicians. He's singing better than ever. The pressure's not just on me." **NOEL (2002)**

" **I never got my head round 'Wonderwall' until I went to see Ryan Adams play and he did an amazing cover of it. So I'm going to cover one of my own songs in the style of Ryan Adams.** "

NOEL (2003)

" We'd forgotten about recording it ('Lyla'), so we hastily cobbled together my original demo and did a bit more work on it, mixed it, and it's come out pretty well. But it's not a fair representation of the album to me. It's not even like the fifth or sixth best track on the album, but it's the most radio-friendly. So we're basically saying we don't get to choose our own singles anymore; it's something I will be addressing before I sign a new record deal. "

NOEL (2005)

" **We will only do a best of when we split up. The only thing we've got that might be in the pipeline next year will be another B-sides album, all the B-sides from 'Standing …' to this lot.** "

NOEL (2005)

THE RECORDS

Behind The Image

❝If we're the wildest fuckin' rock'n'roll band in the country, then British music must be in a pretty sorry state.❞ **NOEL (1994)**

❝We're definitely not the bunch of hard twats that we're made out to be. People can say what they want about Oasis, but we all know that we're not constant 24 hours of the fucking day hooligans. We ain't rock'n'rollers, either. That's people who wear leather kecks, people like Bobby Gillespie. Don't wash their hair for a couple of weeks, wear boots and cowboy hats and think they're American. That's a rock'n'roller. That ain't us.❞ LIAM (1994)

❝Even when I'm really happy I don't smile. People call me miserable all the time, even when I'm not. They shouldn't judge a book by the cover though, should they?❞ **LIAM (1995)**

❝We're the best 'cos we're real. We're not into it for the hype. We just play the songs – we don't act, we just do it. What you see is what you get with us, and that's what you need in indie these days. But we're not an indie band. We're a rock band, pal.❞

LIAM (1995)

❝We're supposed to have an attitude. But attitude never sold a record... If attitude sold records, then drug dealers would be Number 1 all the time because they've got sub-machine guns and that's loads more attitude than me.❞ **NOEL (1995)**

"If you're not into music, you'd find my life quite boring because that's what I'm totally immersed in. Oh, and I like watching football! The odd party, now and again. But generally, it's all music." NOEL (1997)

"My favourite book is The Lion, The Witch and The Wardrobe. I like it. I like that thing of just going into a wardrobe.**"** LIAM (1997)

"Jazz is fucking shit. Jazz is fucking stupid." LIAM (1997)

"Knebworth was top, but I wouldn't do it again. There's too much flying about in fucking helicopters with those gigs. I don't like flying: it's fucking petrifying.**"** NOEL (1997)

❝You start to dress very differently in your thirties. Sometimes, I have to have a long hard look in the mirror and ask myself: 'Do I look a cunt?'❞ NOEL (2004)

❝It's the first time I'm gonna be at home on my own, and I'm really looking forward to not having any (Christmas) cards or decorations up. Christmas day itself I find the longest, most depressing day in the year.**❞ NOEL (2002)**

❝I don't think I'm ordinary because I'm not. I'm special because I'm very, very talented.❞ NOEL (2003)

NOEL WITH SARA McDONALD

Taking On The Tabloids

"I don't see how the tabloids could get any worse for me, unless they claimed I'd had anal sex with an alien, for example: 'Liam Gallagher was caught last night bending an alien across a pool table and poking his bottom.' What more can they say about me?**"**

LIAM (1997)

"Bad boy!" "He takes drugs." "Bad boy!" "Fucking hell - he gets in fights." "Bad boy!" "He's in that rock'n'roll band." "Bad boy!" Fuckin' mad! All those press - I've got 'em in the bag. All the tabloids. In my back pocket. No problem!**"** LIAM (1997)

OASIS Talking

"Do I look as if I can deal with it? (tabloid harassment) Of course, I can deal with it. I can deal with anything. Easy-peasy!" **LIAM (1997)**

"It (tabloid harassment) can get right on top of you, making you ill, do your head in. It's shit, isn't it. People hanging about outside your house every day. Who gives a fuck?" LIAM (1997)

"Them lot (tabloids), I think they fancy me. I think they're all gay. That's what I think anyway."

LIAM (1997)

"Liam's always in the tabloids. But I couldn't tell you the last time he was in there and I couldn't tell you what it was about. There are more important things to worry about in life. If it isn't musical, I don't give a shit." NOEL (2003)

"I know, deep down, that all this photograph-slapping, the fuckin' this and fuckin' that, it's all a front." **NOEL (2005)**

Brothers In Arms...
The Fans

"This girl followed us round to every date and she kept on giving me all this Gaultier stuff. A suit one night, then a shirt or whatever. By the end of the tour, I had like a whole shop's worth." NOEL (1995)

"There was one guy who came to a couple of our gigs and just stood there staring at us. One afternoon I saw him at a soundcheck and went over to ask what he wanted. He said: 'I love you guys, I love your band. Do you want to know how much?' Then he pulled up his sleeve and he had a huge oasis tattooed on his arm – palm trees, water, sand dunes, the lot. So we invited him backstage and he's going: 'I can't believe I'm really sitting here having a beer with the Gallagher brothers.'
"Then someone started slagging his tattoo saying it was only felt-penned on and he got really mad. Suddenly I thought: 'What are we doing? This guy could be a fuckin' psycho. He's probably going to stab me any minute now.'" NOEL (1994)

"We're on the plane over to Japan and all these records and T-shirts appear – ours – young kids wanting autographs, so we end up in a signing thing, and we're just on the fuckin' plane!" LIAM (1994)

"On the Monday morning after our two nights at Earls Court, I'm getting up about 11, in me boxer shorts, having something to eat in the kitchen, when I look up and there's this procession of kids coming down the stairs. I've always sworn I'll never refuse an autograph or whatever, so I open the door and say, 'Do you want a cup of tea, then?' I swear to God, man, it was like the chimps' tea party in here, all these kids, me with the Tetleys and the kettle." NOEL (1996)

"A load of the Manchester City players have been to our gigs. And we got a fax off Francis Lee when 'Some Might Say' went to Number 1. There's a box in the new stand at Maine Road and it's going to be called the Oasis Hospitality Suite." **NOEL (1995)**

"It's weird. If you took a kid from the Bronx and a kid from Brixton who probably have absolutely nothing in common whatsoever, the one thing they'd have in common is they'd own a copy of *Morning Glory*. That's something to be proud of – and we are."

NOEL (1996)

"We're celebrating (with the ten year anniversary tour). We're our own biggest fans anyway and we're going on the road to celebrate the fact that we're fucking mega." **NOEL (2001)**

"They'll (the fans today) be cool man, like they always were. Some of 'em might have a couple of fooking kids, who gives a fook, man? You can still be cool with kids and you can still be cool when you're fooking 50; I don't give a shit. I tell you what: I hope hardly any celebrities turn up, 'cos I don't give a shit, knowwhatImean? I don't want all the so-called cool people backstage at our gigs 'cos they're all fooking knobs." LIAM (2001)

"We're doing two nights at Radio City Music Hall (New York) later this year, and the last time we were there, there was loads of the fucking Mob turning up, because apparently they're big Oasis fans. So there's this big block of seats, and it's all guys with suits and sunglasses... I was looking out for Tony Soprano down the front."

NOEL (2001)

Up In The Sky... Ambition, Success & Arrogance

❝We write music for the guy who walks down the street to get his copy of the *Daily Mirror* and his twenty Bensons everyday, and he's got fuck all going for him, he's got no money. Even if somebody can't afford to buy our record, if they put on the radio while they're cleaning the house, and whistle a song and go, 'Fucking hell, did you hear that tune?' That's what it's all about.❞ NOEL (1994)

❝I know we're flavour of the month or the year or whatever, but a year ago I knew exactly what I wanted us to be doing up to this Christmas. So far it's all going to plan. We wanted to get the album out and to release a single every three months. All those great bands like The Beatles and The Jam used to put out a single every three months no matter where they were touring in the world.❞ NOEL (1994)

❝Progression is going forwards. Going backwards is regression. Going sideways is just aggression.❞ NOEL (1994)

❝There's this thing about a white rock band from England coming over and 'breaking' America – why should there be that weight put around every young band's neck?❞ NOEL (1995)

"I wanted to be in a band because of people like The Beatles and The Stone Roses. By the time we put our first single out I knew we could at least be better than the Roses. We were about making classics, man.**"**

LIAM (1995)

"You can't argue with the songs. It's the whole music business thing that gets in the way. If we had any sort of masterplan it was to keep as much control as possible over our own destiny. We didn't want other people fucking it up for us. That's why we made sure the people around us were people we trusted, people who were on our wavelength. We didn't want hangers-on. And I think that worked." NOEL (1995)

"I'm not particularly arsed about America, but if we could do the same there as we've done in England…. Actually the big dream is to be U2 – not a little Brit-Pop phenomenon with the right clothes and trendy haircuts, which is what we are now.**" NOEL (1996)**

LIAM WITH BONO AND THE EDGE   **AMBITION, SUCCESS & ARROGANCE**

"Because we were big-mouths when we started it, we're gonna have to pull it off now! I don't actually know what the biggest band in the world means. I just want to be as big as we can be and I don't want to leave any avenue unventured. We just want to do anything that's in our power and not have any regrets, never think, 'Oh, we should have done this or we should have done that.' We just want to do everything that's put in front of us as long as it's right. I just want to make great records.

"The biggest band in the world means playing the biggest gigs and I'm not really interested in that. But it comes with selling shitloads of records, so... We want it all. And we want it now."

NOEL (1996)

"All I ever wanted is to fulfil the talent I know I've got. If we ever quit, what will bug me the most is if I never gave it a really good go. If I never pushed myself to realise my potential. I'm fucking there for it. If I fail, then I fail. But I'll know I had a go at it."

NOEL (1996)

RADIOHEAD

"Is there anyone around I find threatening to Oasis? No. Travis are OK. Embrace might be all right if their vocalist starts getting some singing lessons. It's good to see The Verve returning. Radiohead are all right. They could do with speeding up some of their songs but I love the music and the sound of their records. Yeah, if Oasis and Radiohead are the world's two most important bands, that'll do me." NOEL (1997)

"I don't see myself doing this at 50 but I don't see it ending in five years either. Looking back on it all, I wouldn't change anything, really. Even with all the shit we've been through and all the lies they write about us in the press. It all adds up to the overall thing which is the creating of this great mythical rock band. Which is what we are. I mean, I live a life that most people wouldn't be able to imagine. Same with the rest of the band. We're quite happy, generally. All the time, really.**" NOEL (1997)**

"We'll never break up. We'll just call it a day, shake hands, say, 'That was nice. Don't you owe me a royalty cheque?' And that'll be it. We'll go down the pub, say, 'That was great!', and get on with the next thing." LIAM (1997)

"I can't see anyone achieving the success that we've had. I can't see it happening again. What happened to us over the last two years has been a one-off phenomenon. I don't even think we'll match what's happened over the last two years.**" NOEL (1997)**

"If you'd asked on December 3rd 1997 whether I thought Oasis would be around to celebrate their 10th birthday, I'd have laughed ever so politely in your face and said, 'No fucking way, mate.'" NOEL (2001)

"I love Oasis, I love my band, our band's fucking great, the best band in the world when we want to be. But when we want to be we can be fucking idiots. When we put our heads together we are the fucking bollocks and no one can come near us.**" LIAM (2001)**

AMBITION, SUCCESS & **ARROGANCE**

Stepping Out...
Oasis On Stage

❝Are mid-gig scuffles common? Yeah, sort of. He asks me stupid questions. It's like, 'What the hell are you asking me that for? Just get on with the gig!'❞ **NOEL (1994)**

❝**Regardless of what anybody else might think, Oasis have never, ever gone onstage high or drunk. I can't do it, I've never tried to do it, and I never wanna do it. I know, I've tried at rehearsals.**❞

NOEL (1995)

❝Would you put your lighters away? You're not at Elton John.❞

NOEL DURING 'WONDERWALL' AT THE EARLS COURT GIG (1995)

❝**Why don't I move on stage? 'Cos I don't feel as if I have to. I'm not into it. Everyone jumps around, it's boring. Plus, if you dance about you look shit – and I will NOT look shit.**❞ LIAM (1995)

❝George Michael's been coming to loads of our gigs. And then there's people like Bono. He was at Earls Court, then I saw him again in Paris and he goes, 'All right, son.' I said, 'I'm not your son, mate.' I mean, he's done a few good records, but what we're doing now pisses on U2. 'My son?' Fuck off.❞ **LIAM (1995)**

❝**The critics are on about me being on a power trip and wallowing in the limelight, aren't they? Well, I first played it when we went to Japan and we were contracted to play for an hour and a half**

OASIS *Talking*

when we only had a 40-50 minutes set. The one way out was for me to play acoustic. I'll admit to you right now it felt really good. I thought, 'All right, I'll carry on doing this.'

66 But I've had a lot of shit off the band about it. The way I see it is this: I believe the fans of the band would get a chance to see how these songs are born. They all start with one man sitting in a chair with an acoustic guitar singing into a Walkman. I'll never let it go now. 99 NOEL (1996)

66 Earls Court was fucking unbelievable. I think we froze a bit at Glastonbury. I know I did, personally. Halfway through the gig I thought we didn't really want to be there. I thought it was unfair that we were put under that much pressure to pull the whole festival off and, when it didn't happen, people were slagging us off for it. But after the first night at Earls Court... I even surprised meself with how good it was and how good we all played.

66 So now we do these big gigs to tens of thousands of people and we might as well play in our own front-room, man, because we're just totally at ease with it. 99 **NOEL (1996)**

66 The band is absolutely fucking rocking. We're playing the longest we've ever done I think. It's approaching two hours and I think we only play four singles. It's a proper fan's set. If anyone's just remotely coming along for a night out then forget it, 'cos you won't hear anything you know. It's all b-sides and album tracks. The encore will be old favourites, but of the 24/25 songs we've been doing, only four or five are singles. 99 NOEL (2001)

We bypassed the big theatres, we went from nightclubs to stadiums. The Apollo's the only venue in Manchester we've never played. NOEL (2001)

I was like, 'If we're gonna mark ten years of the band let's play places we've never played before' and they were like, 'You've played everywhere!' and I went, 'Well we haven't played the Apollo'. You know, you do lose something when you play outdoors because you go on in daylight and it's great for the spectacle, but there's nothing better than seeing a band indoors in the dark and it's fucking loud as fuck, proper rocking and sweaty. NOEL (2001)

They were fantastic (Gem and Andy playing their first real Oasis gig). It was good for me, too, because I always felt that, before, if I had an off-night playing guitar then the whole thing would fall apart because Bonehead and Guigs weren't the best musicians in the world. But now Gem plays more lead than I do, which is brilliant because I can concentrate on the singing. It just feels fucking really good, it gives you more confidence. NOEL (2001)

I wanted to play Wembley Stadium, I always have done. I don't know. I just thought, I don't want to play fucking Hamburg but I want to play fucking Wembley, d'ya know what I mean? I just felt I owed it to the kids here, because this is where we come from and they were the ones that fucking made us. No disrespect to anybody in Europe or anything, but if you sell out Wembley Stadium for two nights in two days, six weeks before the album comes out, you've got an obligation to play for them people. NOEL (2001)

Festival Fever

❝I've been (to the V Festival) a few times and only ever seen one good gig – that was the Coral a few years ago. I'm looking forward to it, it's the only festival we're doing in England this year. I think it could be good craic. I am a bit concerned about the kind of crowd we'll get – it's all *EastEnders* extras and fucking D-list celebrities all there for a day out. Cat Deeley and all that.❞

NOEL (2005)

❝**Apart from Maroon 5 all the bands on the bill are friends of ours. There's The Stands, Jet, The Zutons, The La's and us on the same stage. So our backstage area will be great.**❞ NOEL (2005)

❝You can count out all the festivals in England. I don't think we've ever pulled it off for some reason. Maybe this time. The thing is, when we're playing festivals abroad, we're usually second on the bill – we never get to headline. Whenever we're headlined Glastonbury, by the time we get on everybody's twatted.

I remember the last one we did in Australia was fantastic, because we were second on the bill to some band we'd never fucking heard of. We blew them offstage every night, it was great. And there was one festival we did in Switzerland on the *Heathen Chemistry* tour, and they said we were that good, they were convinced we were miming.❞ **NOEL (2005)**

"Fuck it, who wants to stay clean if it's muddy? Fucking join in, have a laugh. It doesn't really matter. Ian McCulloch's the only type of person who'll walk round in white trousers looking like a lunatic." NOEL (2005)

"Who the fuck wears white parkas (at Glastonbury) anyway? – Him (Liam), Ian McCulloch and Paul Weller. He likes his concrete, Liam.**" NOEL (2005)**

"Best place to have sex? In somebody else's tent."

NOEL (2005)

"Tent or Tourbus? Tourbus, without a doubt. You can get 16 people on a tourbus, you can leave at any point, you've got a proper bed, and a fridge, and telly to watch the football. Say no more.**"**

NOEL (2005)

"I fucking hate Glastonbury, mate. I'm only here for the money. It's fucking shit. I've got to wear fucking wellies." LIAM (2005)

Oasis On Tour

"Japan is the best place ever. Best people, man... Fucking mega. It totally blew my head, and everyone else's. Getting chased round shopping precincts... It was man, like a fucking *Hard Day's Night*, man. The tour bus is stuffed with presents, loads of records, dead dear Beatles stuff, purple fucking vinyl and that... Loads of footballs with our lyrics written on 'em but done different!**"**

LIAM (1994)

" Most of the nights seem to end in some sort of chaos, but compared to things that have happened in the past, the last tour has been pretty easy.**"** NOEL ON AMERICAN TOUR (1995)

" We haven't really stopped over the last year. Half the time we don't even know we're playing anywhere until we see the adverts and the sold out signs. I don't think we've had more than a week off in a year and a half.**"** NOEL (1995)

"We played in Atlanta on this tour and everyone was mad for it. They were hanging like bats from the ceiling and flying off the stage. It was fucking weird." LIAM (1995)

" The Whiskey-A-Go-Go (in LA) was the worst gig we've ever played. Afterwards, I said to the others, 'I don't want to do this if you're not going to put everything you've got into it...' Everyone just kind of looked around and no one said anything, so I thought, 'Fuck it, we're splitting up'. I got $800 in cash that was the tour money and I got on the first plane out of LA. I had half an ounce of coke and I thought, 'Right, I'm having this, then I'm going back to England. It's over'.

" On the way, though, I was reading through a copy of *Melody Maker* and saw the advert for all these Oasis gigs in England and they were sold out. I didn't even know we were supposed to be playing half of them. Anyway, I saw the sold out signs and I thought that if I'd been one of the people who'd bought tickets and the band had cancelled, I'd have thought Oasis were complete bastards. I knew I should go back to the others and we should sort it out.**"** NOEL (1995)

"He went off on one. When you're out in America doing all the record company stuff 24 hours a day, everything just goes mad. It probably did need sorting out, though. And it was." LIAM (1995)

" I didn't come all the way over (to America) to shake hands with some knobhead executive's wife.**"** NOEL (1995)

"I really miss home. I'm mad for seeing my mam. Mad for it. I've been away so long!" LIAM (1994)

OASIS ON STAGE

"The dangerous thing was just being so busy you wake up one morning and you forget where you are, which country you're in and what you're supposed to be doing there. Then you think, 'Oh! I've been doing this for so long that I can't remember when I started and I don't know when I'm going to stop.'" **NOEL (1997)**

"We'd just been touring for too long. We'd been touring for three years. Sick of playing the same songs over and over again."
NOEL (1997)

"I love it, man! Wait 'til we go on this fooking little tour round England; I fooking can't wait. I'm on the bus, man. I'm gonna send me mam on holiday that week!" **LIAM (2001)**

"I could put my professional hat on and I could say that it's really important to come and play for these people for the social aspect of Rock In Rio. Or I could be honest and say it's fucking really cold in England and it's really warm here." NOEL (2000)

"You might have heard I had a little accident (taxi collision in Indianapolis). Well, you know how many get well cards I got? Fuckin' one. If this was 1995 and I was selling lots of records, then I'd be gettin' loads of good wishes. My record company didn't even send flowers!" **NOEL (2002)**

"It was my first car crash. Nothing flashed before my eyes! Not a fucking thing! It only lasted a couple of seconds. It'd take a lot longer than that for my life to flash by, man!" NOEL (2002)

"The longer you do it (touring), the more you do fear it. At some point, you've got to accept that music has moved on and you're not the cat's whiskers any more." **NOEL (2004)**

"I think Oasis only really make sense if it's played in front of 50,000 people. I think if it's played in a pub it wouldn't make much sense. Size is an important part of Oasis." NOEL (2004)

The States & Americans

❝America's big and weird and fucking huge and it frightens the life out of me. It takes me time to get me head around it. New York's cool, I think LA's shit. Chicago's cool and San Francisco too. If we break America, cool. We'll still go there whether we do or not. But we need to take it easy. I'm sick of all this running around. Just hold your horses, put the brakes on a little bit. Noel doesn't want to, but I do.

❝There's no point in blitzing America. Whatever is meant to happen in this walk of like, man, will happen. Whatever will be, will be. Why be in a band if we're all going to end up in the cuckoo farm?❞

LIAM (1996)

❝Americans don't buy enough of our records! They don't buy enough concert tickets! It's too big and tours take too long and we usually get on each other's nerves after three weeks.❞

NOEL (1997)

OASIS ON STAGE

"A lot of people have said we've cracked America but I don't think we have and I'm not particularly bothered whether we do or not. I'm not interested in having an aeroplane or anything like that. I don't have the parking space for it." NOEL **(1997)**

"It's not about going to America to crack it anymore. We just do things because we want to, not because we have to." NOEL (1997)

"All bands go there for about two weeks, do four gigs and then come home. We ended up going over there for two months, doing shitloads of gigs and that, and you just get bored, and you start getting pissed. All the rows that ever started, we've been drunk: 'Look at your shoes, you dick'; 'Who are you calling dick?'; 'Calling you a dick'; 'Who's a dick'... and before you know it, it's (shouts as if hailing a cab) 'Concorde!' It's all to do with lager, isn't it? (Points at can.) That is evil shit, man!" NOEL **(1997)**

"Americans don't get it. There was a point where everything we did was (New York drawl) 'incredible'. 'God, the way you guys walked onstage was just incredible! The way you tuned that guitar between "Don't Look Back In Anger" and "Live Forever" was fucking incredible!' It's like, 'Shut the fuck up, man! We're not even that good live, for fuck's sake, let alone incredible. We're pissed up half the time.' 'Your dressing room's incredible! Look at that rider - it's incredible!' Fucking wankers."

NOEL (1997)

“Americans want grungy fucking people, stabbing themselves in the head on stage. They get a bright bunch like us, with deodorant on, they don’t get it.” **LIAM (1997)**

“**There was one gig where I got fucking bladdered before and I was pissed up, rolling about on stage, on me knees doing that (satanic metal pose), with me tongue out, and they were going fucking mental. That’s how stupid they are. These lot are going, ‘Get him back in the dressing room, he’s pissed as an arse.’ But they were mad for it. That’s when you’ve got to go, ‘What time’s the next flight, man?’”** NOEL (1997)

“No offence, but to be as big as U2 are in the States, you’ve got to be prepared to sell your arse a little bit. You get to the point where you don’t want to make another video, or meet the owner of Sam Goody’s Records in Cincinnati. Bono wants to be the biggest rock star in the world, which is why he is.” **NOEL (2001)**

"What a fucking waste! Of life! There's gonna be a race war. You just fear for sanity... You know what they're like in the Midwest, fucking old Chip polishing his old M16 he uses to kill deer sat watching it thinking, 'Right! Where's the nearest fucking Arab?' Religious fanatics, you can't argue with these people. Nostradamus. George Bush's dad is just gonna be, 'Son? This is your destiny!' Well, it's the end of the world, innit? At the end of the day, fuck 'em. They're all mad! No wonder we fucking take drugs! It's just fucking... fucking... spectacularly fucked up! Right! Get me on the front of this fucking paper before it all goes pear-shaped." NOEL (2001)

"It's like they can't do without the doughnuts and the coffee and all that. So we got into a huddle in the corner and said, 'Do we really wanna go (recording in California)?' Because it's like that scene in *Star Wars* when the little ship flies into the Death Star. It's kinda like that with us." NOEL (2005)

"This is the longest time I've spent in America without anything going tits-up, which is incredible." NOEL (2005)

"There's gonna be us and Jet and Kasabian (on a US tour). That's gonna be fucking mental. I'm gonna need to have a liver transplant when I get back. It's gonna be good, though, I can't wait."

NOEL (2005)

"The reason U2 and R.E.M. and Coldplay are the biggest white rock bands in America is because of their frontmen. Not being negative towards Liam, he's just not Chris Martin, he's not Bono, he's not Michael Stipe. He's Liam. For all intents and purposes, Americans don't get Liams." NOEL (2005)

Over The Top...
Violent
Tendencies

"If someone wants to cause me harm, it doesn't matter how big they are, I'll smash 'em up. I'm mad for it.**"** LIAM (1995)

"It was a really good atmosphere until the middle of 'Bring It On Down'. Then I was doing my guitar solo and a guy just appeared and he was about two foot away from me and I thought he was a stagediver. He had this big ring on and he just smacked me in the eye. When somebody does that you don't think of being a pop star or being in a band or the audience, you just want to retaliate.
"I've got a bit of a headache, a bit of a lump gathering over my eye but if I have another 75 cigarettes and a couple of bottles of gin I'll be sort of all right, I might go to sleep tonight." NOEL (1994)

"People think we're up for a fight and that, but we're not up for a fight. We didn't start it, we're here to play songs, that's what we're about. We're not about fighting. We want to do the songs, do the set and get off. But if someone gets up and thinks he's a bit hard and goes for it he's going to get it.
"I can't understand the mentality of somebody who wants to go and pay money to go into a gig to smack one of the band. It sets a precedent... We've been saying for a year to our record company and our manager that we need more security and it's all 'We can't afford it'. But does it take someone to lose an eye to get security?**"** LIAM (1994)

OASIS *Talking*

Page 143

"People have got to respect our position. Music, and the fans of the band, it's the be all and end of it. But I've only got two eyes, one goes and I don't get one back. At the end of the day it's only rock'n'roll but I'm not prepared to die." NOEL (1994)

"We had to drive out of that gig down a side street with three hundred people lined up along the pavement, and they just smashed the van to bits. Why play for a load of fuckin' monkeys, man? We don't know how we should be acting at the moment. Hopefully all this'll pass." NOEL (1994)

"Everything just went mad. People were smashing bottles and throwing things all over the place. At one point, someone opened a window and just started to lob everything out. I woke up the next morning, looked out of the window and the car park was, like, full of bedrooms. It was a laugh. I'm not saying it's fucking important or anything, but, you know…" LIAM ON HOTEL TRASHING (1994)

"Those plate glass windows are just saying, 'Throw a chair through me.'" NOEL (1995)

"On the last American tour I was in hospital in Detroit with chest pains 'cos I'd gone really over the top and stayed up for nearly three days. We were in Chicago and we heard 'Cigarettes And Alcohol' had gone in at seven, and at that point we realised how big we were. So we had this party and I'd been up for two days previous and I always had this mad theory that if anyone could break the 72-hour barrier they'd never need to sleep again. And, of course, that's not true 'cos I ended up in fucking hospital. I stayed up for 76 hours and spent the next 72 in hospital. But nobody said nothing to me. It was only the day after that I said to myself, 'You fucking idiot, you can't do this'. I'm definitely not as mad as I was." NOEL (1995)

"It's typical of Liam. Seven in the morning on Oxford Street, two policemen ask him what he's up to and instead of being polite he says, 'What's it got to do with you, cuntybollocks?'" NOEL (1997)

"I will beat the fookin' livin' daylight shit out of them. That goes for George (Harrison), (Mick) Jagger, (Keith) Richards and that other cunt (Paul McCartney) that gives me shit... If any of them old farts have got a problem with me, then leave yer Zimmer frames at home and I'll hold you up with a good right hook. They're jealous and senile and not gettin' enough meat pies. If they want to fight, I'll beat them up." LIAM (1997)

"Anyone who jumps on our stage has got it. And anyone who wants to jump on our stage will get it. Not from me, from Terry (man-mountain minder). Them hooligans got it.**" LIAM (1997)**

"Do you think you're going to get a fucking bunch of people in a room and they're not gonna heckle? Because I'm the biggest monkey in the world and I'll fucking heckle my balls off."

LIAM (2001) AT Q AWARDS

"I was having Sunday lunch with mum and Nic (Appleton, girlfriend) and this geezer comes over and says could he have a word? It's important. He said he had some information which needed to be passed on - I knew he was a loon because he had a Bible. He said that John Lennon was the last person to know about it and that he was sent to pass it on to me. I said, 'Fuck off, get out of here!' He said this information would make my jaw drop. So I said, 'Look, if you don't get the fuck out of here, man, see that? (points to his fist), That'll make your fucking jaw drop. So fuck off, you cunt!'**"**

LIAM (2001)

❝I've only been down Oxford Street once. It was a few years ago after an awards ceremony. It was three in the morning. And I got arrested. The only time I ever see the street is from a car. I spend my whole life being driven around.**❞** LIAM (2002)

❝All I'm bothered about is that he (Liam) can still sing. Liam's got his teeth back for Christmas and we're back in business.**❞**

NOEL (2002)

❝It's always the same. It starts off great and then somewhere, usually in America, I don't know why... probably the sight of cactus plants or something like that... it freaks Liam out. Then he oversteps the mark a little bit and... it degenerates from there. It starts out great, then it just ends up being a bit of a shame really.**❞** NOEL (2005)

VIOLENT TENDENCIES

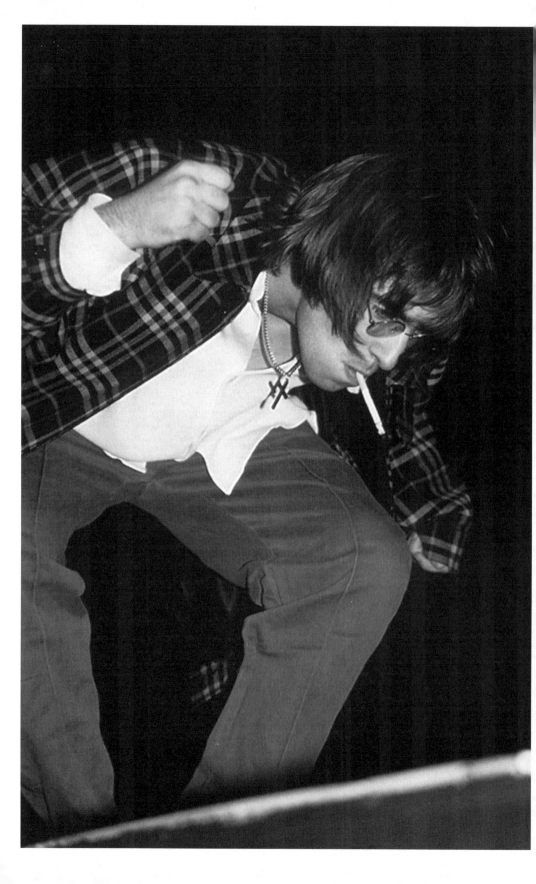

Oasis
Outs & Ins

“The problems started almost from the beginning of *Definitely Maybe*. It wasn't with the band, apart from our drummer, who's Ringo Starr incarnate and can't keep time to save his fucking life. (Producer) Dave Bachelor was trying to be clever. We're a rock'n'roll band and he was separating everything out, doing it clean and it was sounding too produced.

“I'm saying, 'Let's get a bit mad here, let's really let go and be young and compress the shit out of this so that the speakers blow up.' He'd go, 'Nope, 'cos this is the way we done it in our day, son.' I thought either we go with his saneness or my madness, and I'm in charge so, 'sorry mate, you've got to go.'”

NOEL (1994) ON GETTING RID OF THEIR PRODUCER

“We've got where we wanted to be, but it's been fucking hard work. There was a lot of traumas along the way, on tours, in America, getting shot of the drummer and all the rest of it... So it's not been as big a laugh as we thought it'd be.” NOEL (1995)

“It had been building up for ages. Tony (McCarroll) had to go. And it was obviously best to do it before we started recording the second album. Getting Alan (White) in meant that we had this whole new freedom. He's a top drummer and you'd have to be really stupid not to recognise the difference he makes. And his old man really *is* a dustman. Blur will probably try and steal him.”

NOEL (1995)

OASIS *Talking*

"When we got rid of Tony we didn't have a replacement drummer and everyone was going, 'You idiot, what are you going to do about the album?' because it was just before we were meant to start recording. And I was the only one who'd heard the songs because we don't do demos or any of that shit and I knew, well, I like Tony as a geezer, but he wouldn't have been able to drum the new songs. People can say, 'Oh you didn't give him a chance', and I didn't." NOEL (1995)

GUIGSY

"Alan's the new Keith Moon. He's a Charlton fan and he was taught drums by the best drummer in England." **NOEL (1995)**

"Alan's great. We'd sit and watch him at soundchecks. I mean, nobody ever watches the drummer at soundchecks, especially not in our band. But he'd be doing stuff and we'd be going, 'How'd he do that'?"

NOEL (1995)

"I don't want to slag Guigys and Bonehead off, but them leaving and Gem and Andy coming in has been the saving of Oasis. I know you're thinking 'Gallagher's talking through his arse again', but wait till you hear the new album!"

NOEL (2001)

BONEHEAD

"We went to France to record because we were trying to get Liam off the drink. It makes recording a really difficult thing to do when he's pissed. So I said, No one can drink while we're there, because it won't be fair on Liam. I said I would kick it in the head for three months. We needed to give him all the support we could; everyone agreed to lay off it. But Bonehead would go off on the piss. I said, 'You're just rubbing it in his face; if I'm not drinking then no cunt is.' So we'd all be there drinking water and Bonehead would be knocking back the red wine.

"I politely asked him to give it a rest and he told me to fuck off. Then there was an argument. So he said, 'That's it, I'm off!' and went back to England. I think he thought we'd say, 'Don't leave.' But we thought... hang on a minute! So we said if you wanna leave you'd better make an announcement, and he did."

NOEL (2000)

"All that romantic notion about Oasis being a gang was all bullshit. I lived in London on my own for two years, the rest of the band lived in Manchester. It was never a gang. I never hung out with them, they never hung out with me. We never had the same circle of friends. We never drank in the same places. I was always a bit of a loner anyway." NOEL (2000)

"The backing-tracks are pretty much done and we're going to add strings and things next week. Liam, being a law unto himself, turns up at four o'clock in the morning and Alan, whose twin loves are cars and drinking,

OUTS & **INS**

buggers off as soon as his drum parts are done.
Which used to leave me in the studio with Bonehead and
Guigsy, who I didn't have more than an hour's worth of
conversation with in seven years.

❝Now that Andy and Gem are there getting all enthusiastic about
stuff, it's a far more pleasurable experience. Song-wise, Liam's
got three, Andy and Gem have two each and I've come up with
the rest. I'm artistically, morally, contractually and everything
else obliged to say this, but I honestly think it'll be as good as
Morning Glory and *Definitely Maybe*.❞ NOEL (2001)

❝I felt hurt (by Bonehead leaving) because if he's got a problem,
which I don't think he had, with the band, then he should've been
able to speak to us about it. 'Cos we'd been in it so long I thought
we were that fucking close. When we were together, the band,
we talked about things. If I had a problem with the band, I'd say it.
If Noel did, and if Whitey did, they did say it. And I just feel a bit
gutted that (Bonehead and Guigsy) mustn't have felt like we were
mates, or something, that they couldn't come out and go,
'Oh, I got a problem.'❞ **LIAM (2000)**

ANDY BELL

❝Now Andy and Gem and Liam are writing I don't have that same sort of pressure. It's just a question of getting this year out of the way and getting enough songs together to make another record.❞ NOEL (2001)

❝Gem was in the band about three weeks before Andy so they didn't come in together. We'd known Gem for years from him being on Creation. We had about three weeks where three or four bass players came in - that was like a week before we had to go to America and do these radio shows, which would have been last November.Then Liam was reading *Melody Maker* on the way to rehearsals one day and he said, 'Fucking Andy Bell's joining Gay Dad!' and I was like, 'Oh, right', and he said, 'Why don't we get him to play bass?' And I said, 'I don't think he plays bass.' So Liam said, 'Fucking hell, if he can play guitar he can play bass.' I thought it was a good idea, and a couple of days later he came over. Once the five of us got in the room and played the tunes it was just fucking spot on. He looked the part too.❞ **NOEL (2001)**

GEM

❝We went for a curry with Gem and asked him to join the band. That was it. It wasn't like a fucking job interview - he knew what he had to do and he enjoys it.❞ LIAM (2001)

❝For me it's straight down the line: if they (Bonehead and Guigsy) don't want to be in the band and don't want to play with you then fuck off, see you later. That's what it's about - you're not married to them, are you? It was their band as much as it was ours and if they're not giving fucking 100 per cent then see you later.❞

LIAM (2001)

OUTS & INS

"When we did those radio shows it was great because it was the first time we'd got to that drunken five o'clock in the morning situation, talking about music and all that. Andy's 'Stones, Stones, Stones' all the time and Liam's 'Beatles, Beatles, Beatles'. There was like a fucking Mexican stand-off one night in a bar. After we got past that one we knew it was going to be fine. When we started rehearsing for the tour it was just amazing." NOEL (2001)

"They've (Bonehead and Guigsy) never actually spoken to me since they left the band I don't know why. I suppose it was weird for Liam because those three were really close and I'd usually be doing my own thing, writing or doing interviews.**"** **NOEL (2001)**

"Well, I rang them last Christmas. Every now and then Bonehead will ring me up and go, 'Fucking hell, I'm fucking doing this, I'm fucking doing that.' But I'm like, (disdainfully) 'Really, really?' I've got nothing in common with them any more. We never hung out with them anyway. The only time I saw them was when we were on tour. The only thing I had in common with them was the music and now they're not in the band any more. I wish them all the best." LIAM (2001)

"Really, I'm not interested in why they did it (Guigsy and Bonehead leaving). I couldn't care less what they're doing. As far as I'm concerned they're not in the band. They don't exist.**"** **NOEL (2000)**

"As soon as we made the decision to carry on it was like, we've got a fucking album, we've got the tour and we've got to go and do it. It was just a case of getting the right people in, and we have. Now it's like we've never had anybody else in the band, y'know what I mean? On previous albums I would write the songs and that would be it. Now everybody chips in. Now I'm saying, What do you think of that? Is it the right arrangement?" NOEL (2001)

"I know we'll probably never be as big in this country as we were in '95/'96, but I'm in a band with some brilliant players now and that's never been the case before. We think of Gem as our Ronnie Wood. It's a totally new band. I'm more excited about the future than ever.**"**

NOEL (2001)

"Alan White has been asked to leave Oasis by the other band members. The band's scheduled recording sessions remain unaffected." OFFICIAL OASIS WEBSITE (2004)

"We've known Zak (Starkey) for a while and we asked him if he'd play on a few songs and he said yeah, and he has done and it's been absolutely fantastic.**"** NOEL (2004)

"Zak's first gig will be to 150,000 people. But y'know, he's rehearsing all the Oasis songs now." NOEL (2004)

"People keep asking us why we're doing it ('My Generation') live when we done it on the last tour – well, we're got The Who's drummer (Zak Starkey) on this tour. He plays it properly like Keith Moon, we've kind of made it our own now.**"** NOEL (2005)

NME
NEW MUSICAL EXPRESS
brat
AWARDS
with
Miller
Genuine Draft

Brits, Brats & Ivors...
Awards

"Awards don't come as much of a surprise when you know you deserve them. We just used the ceremonies as an excuse to get off our faces and wind people up. The only awards that matter are when people go out and buy your records. The fans are the most important people to us. The rest is just bullshit.

"It's nice to get all the gold and platinum discs, though. I went to Gracelands and saw this room that Elvis had that was like a tower. It was about 200 feet high and it was covered in discs right up to the ceiling. The rate we're going, we're going to have that many by Christmas. They're going to have to start delivering them in lorries, or something." **NOEL (1995)**

"We should have got even more awards really. There isn't another band in the country who can touch us. And they know it." LIAM (1995)

"Next year when I win (an Ivor Novello songwriting award) I won't turn up – they can give it to me mam instead, cheeky bastards." **NOEL (1995)**

"Would I accept an MBE? Yeah, I would because you could probably flog it. I'd accept but I'd rather he offered me a place in the fucking cabinet. Minister For Rock!

ELVIS PRESLEY

OASIS *Talking*

They've got a Minister For Sport but who gives a fuck about sport, all that bollocks, running around in shorts and that! Fuck that nonsense! I could be the Minister For Rock. Just see myself in the House Of Lords falling asleep and dribbling." NOEL (1995)

"I watched (the 1995 Brit Awards) on telly the next day and I can't remember half of what went on or who was there. We were just completely out of it. I remember this little man coming up to us and saying, 'You're going to have to leave'. I thought we were being thrown out and I said, 'No, mate, you don't understand, I've just won an award.' He said, 'Yeah, I know you have, but you've got to get out. I'm locking up.'" **NOEL (1995)**

"It's hard to be humble at times like this so I won't try. You're all shit." NOEL'S ACCEPTANCE SPEECH AT BRAT AWARDS (1996)

"We all feel justified. There was all that stuff round about the time of 'Roll With It' – people were writing us off and saying this was the first knock-back and we were finished and all that. But we know how good our records are, we know how good our band is and we know how good musicians we are. And I know myself how good a songwriter I am, so I don't have to justify ourselves to anyone except the people." **NOEL (1996) ON WINNING FOUR BRAT AWARDS**

"**I'll accept this (*Q* award for best live act) on behalf of a crap album with crap lyrics.**" NOEL (1996)

"I'm gonna win everything. Best male singer, best female singer, the lot." **NOEL ON THE BRIT AWARDS (1996)**

"**What do I think about the Brits committee? They're a bunch of twats who think people like Sting and Bowie are the cutting edge of music.**" NOEL (1996) AFTER PICKING UP THREE AWARDS

AWARDS "

Over The Horizon...
The Future &
New Beginnings

“There's only so far you can go in this country. Once you've played Wembley Arena, for instance, that's it. Unless you play Wembley Stadium, and, you know, I mean, that's for U2 and fuckin' INXS, not us. It is gonna level out. Hopefully, in a couple of years' time a bunch of kids'll come along like we did when we heard the Roses album. To all intents and purposes, we're equal with them now, and all the others. So it's like, Right then, let's see who is the greatest fuckin' band in England. Y'know, Suede? Take an E, guys! Sort it out!” **NOEL (1994)**

“**Two years ago I told** *Melody Maker* **that 'Whatever' would be a Top Five record round Christmas 1994. I knew it was going to happen. People slag off that belief, start calling it arrogance. What's wrong with arrogance? I know how good we are.**”

NOEL (1995)

“I think of Oasis as, like, five years or something. We can do it and we're going to be the best band in the world, we know it. We can sell loads of records, do what we want to do, then afterwards there'll be loads of time to piss around. I mean, I'm no angel, but right now Oasis means more to me than anything in the world. And if we don't do what I know we can do, I'll regret it forever.” **NOEL (1995)**

“**When this finishes, we will sit back with our consciences clear that we never lied to anyone. That's why I will slag my record company off in public,**

I'll slag Liam off in public and he'll slag me off in public.
We won't hold it all in, because if we're people's favourite band
they should know what that band's about.** NOEL (1995)

**You get all these bands who get a bit of success and then they
go and have a year off! Why? There's all these bands who go,
'Oh, we're having a year off and get our heads together, to find
some fucking perspective or something', and then they come back
and they find that music's moved on so much that the place that
they left has vanished and gone forever.

**So my plan was always that once we got to some place we'd just
keep at it while we were on a roll. I mean, I'm only 28. I can take
a year out when I'm 38. Plus, we get bored after a week or so.
What are we going to do? Lie on a beach, watch fucking telly?
I don't think so.** **NOEL (1995)**

In '95 I wanted everything. And I got most of it. LIAM (1995)

**We're not going to stop until it gets boring. It's been a mad couple
of years, but we're in a position now where we've got more control
over what we do. There's nothing else I'd rather do more than this,
so we're just going to keep on and see where it goes.** **NOEL (1995)**

**I hate to keep using the
words, 'How big we are'
because people just keep
thinking we're just these
success-heads and all that.
But it's only dawning on us
now how important we're
becoming and I suppose it's
going to put a bit of pressure
on us in the long run.
But cometh the hour, cometh
the band. And if there is one
band in the world equipped
to pull it off, man, it's us.**

NOEL (1996)

THE FUTURE & NEW BEGINNINGS

❝Now we're entered into this fucking democracy thing. which is why things take for fucking ever now. I used to be in charge of this band, but now people get upset so it's like 'fine, you look after your shit and I'll look after mine', which is why things take forever.❞

NOEL (2001)

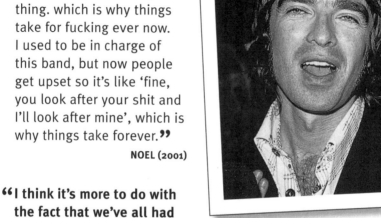

❝**I think it's more to do with the fact that we've all had new starts in our life, you know what I mean. Andy and Gem have just joined the band so for them it's a new adventure, and me and Liam have just left a little episode of our past behind so it's just sparked a new beginning really – but even that sounds a little pretentious for my liking, so don't print that.**❞ NOEL (2001)

❝I can't tell anybody what to do in the band because now it's this new democracy. There's no referee and it looks like it's just going to drift. It'll end up in an almighty fight.❞ **NOEL (2001)**

❝**I have corrected all the mistakes that I have made in my life, getting married to the wrong person and doing too many drugs. But I am still young. I can start again.**❞ NOEL (2001)

❝Everyone else has been writing songs and I've been stung into action a bit. I'm slowing down as a writer, but Liam and Gem and Andy are filling up the gaps. Liam wants to make *Double Fantasy*, Gem wants to make a T. Rex record and Andy's into Buffalo Springfield. The songs I've written are not really what I want for the next record - we really want to make a rock'n'roll record and they're not rock'n'roll songs. So it's a case of demoing as many songs as we can until somebody says, 'We've not had a record out for two years, let's go and fucking do something.'❞ **NOEL (2001)**

"We've been through a lot of shit and we've learned a lot about this group. And what we've learned is that we're still the greatest rock'n'roll band in the world. It doesn't matter what you throw at us, we're going all right. A new line-up, new people, new life - I'm happy." LIAM (2001)

"We would like to make a pure rock 'n' roll record. To record it live, no overdubs, and just get the best performances and put it out like that. Now whether that happens, I don't know. I think we've gotten a bit slow down the years with slow songs and ballads but until we actually get in the studio and turn the tape machine on, we don't know what's gonna happen." NOEL (2000)

Barcelona Barney

"I've had a major disagreement with Monkey Boy, the singer. It's been made virtually impossible for me to tour at the moment because he's been a bit of an idiot. It'll all be sorted out privately at the end of the tour and I'll do my talking to him to his face and not through his mate at *The Sun* like he seems to be doing recently." NOEL (2000)

"I lost it with him. It was a proper fight – it wasn't just like, I'll scratch your eyes out you bitch! It was a proper brawl, and I'm actually quite proud of the fact that it came to blows. He knows if he crosses me that far I'll leave him in the shit."
NOEL (2000)

"Alan had got tendonitis and the doctor came out and said he had to have a few days' rest. So we had to null that gig. We had to wait for the crew to pack the gear down, which was going to take six or seven hours, so we sat in the dressing room drinking and getting really pissed. I can't remember how the argument started, somebody said something about fucking nonsense and then it all escalated into this big ruck between me and (Liam). One by one everyone was leaving the dressing room and I was saying, 'Get fucking back in here, because this concerns all of us!' Then in the end he said something and I ended up smacking him." NOEL (2001)

"He said things about my missus in the heat of the moment. What exactly? I'm not going to tell you, that's between me and him and, of course, the 50 people that were in the dressing room at the time. It was a matter of principle. I couldn't go back onstage and sing harmonies with him after that. I mean, he really fucking hurt me and it was like, either he goes or I go, because if I don't leave then he's not going to respect me as a person. He knows what I'm like. We ended up in a fight, throwing bottles. I got a black eye." NOEL (2001)

"He won the fight but I left my mark. What was it all about? Personal shit and that's got nothing to do with anyone else."

LIAM (2001)

"I actually felt sorry for Andy and Gem because they were sat there thinking, 'What the fuck's gone on there?'" NOEL (2001)

"I think that was probably the worst. It was nothing to do with the band or the music. It was all to do with me and him being fucking knobheads - as usual." LIAM (2001)

"If it had been one of the other guys I'd have laid them out and then probably fired them. But I'm not in a position to do that with Liam, he's my fucking brother." NOEL (2001)

"I stayed over in Barcelona with Whitey on the piss, got to Paris still pissed, check into the hotel and he (Noel)'s in the lobby. I'm like, Right, let's fucking have it again! This is the next day, I'm still wasted, so we had a little bit of a fucking hock and he just got off and that was it - I went to bed and crashed out, woke up the next morning and he was gone." LIAM (2001)

"Liam hurt me pretty fucking bad, emotionally. The only way to get back at him was. If you're going to carry on with the tour, you do it without me." NOEL (2001)

"The first time we actually saw each other (again) was on-stage in fucking Dublin. And what I thought was really fucking cheesy was at the end of 'Acquiesce' (Noel's paean to their fraternal bond), he comes out and fucking puts out his hand, knowing full well that I'm not going to go (whips hand away in spiteful playground fashion). The world media is watching, our mum's in the crowd, and he comes over and shakes hands and that was the big fucking defining moment of the tour. I just thought, fucking hello..." NOEL (2001)

"When I was 26 the most important thing in my entire life was the group and writing songs. But now it's not. I've devoted enough of my time to Oasis. I've given enough, so now I wanna take a bit back. But I never said I was gonna do a solo album and leave the fuckin' band. I just wanna do little things that make it interesting for me. But I've no intention of leaving the band."

NOEL (2000)

Rest... In Peace?

"If the band split up. I wouldn't stop, I'd go on.
I wouldn't just be a singer, I'd carry on as a
guitarist/singer like Lennon. I love him, I love his spirit, I love
it all. I'll never meet him, but I'm as close as could be, just
because I'm totally into what he was all about. It's like 'Live
Forever' – if you get to know yourself, and you get to know your
spirit, your spirit will live forever." LIAM (1994)

"One day I will go and I won't come back. I don't see this going on
forever, even though loads of people do. I don't see it going past...
I see it as three albums and that's it. I don't think I can do any
more with Oasis after that. I think a band like us will have run our
course after that. There's only so many anthems you can write."

NOEL (1995)

"I live for now, not for what happens after I die. If I die and
there's something afterwards, I'm going to hell, not heaven.
I mean, the devil's got all the good gear. What's God got? The
Inspiral Carpets and nuns. Fuck that." LIAM (1995)

"On my grave, I want them to write, 'Don't Fucking Come Here
With Your Bunches Of Flowers.' I don't want a gravestone, I want
a v-sign, two fingers. A really fucking huge v-sign, 20 foot tall or
something. When you're dead, you're dead. It's now that matters."

LIAM (1995)

"Am I planning to go solo? No. This is my first band and my first
rock'n'roll experience and it'll be my last. I mean that from the
bottom of my heart." NOEL (1996)

"I'm not splitting up because some cunt don't like it! No-one can
turn round to me and say 'I'm not into it,' I'm bang into it and he's
(Noel) the same. There's no way I'll be turning like the fooking
Rolling Stones. I don't go on the road to make money - it just so
happens we do - but I go on the road to have a laugh an' play me

THE FUTURE & **NEW BEGINNINGS**

rock'n'roll and that's the fooking end of it, and if anyone tries to tell me any different they're off their fooking tits. I don't wanna be the biggest band in the world any more, I wanna be the best. And we are the fooking best and I truly believe that. He's the best songwriter in the world, end of story and that's all that I can say...**"** LIAM (2001)

"We've never said we're breaking up, though I grant you it did come very close at one point. It's just... this year's been such a fucking weird one, what with the collapse of the label (Creation), all the shit that went on with the tour, then Liam and his missus breaking up, then me and my missus, not to mention all the shit behind the scenes that never gets out. Like, I got a phone call today saying my house in Ibiza has virtually fallen into the fucking sea..." NOEL (2001)

"To be honest, coming back from Spain and going into them stadium gigs, I just thought that (Liam) was becoming a caricature of himself and the band was becoming a parody of itself. But time is a great healer, and speaking to Andy and Gem and Alan they were saying, 'We can't split up' and I was saying, We're not going to split up, I'm going to leave. I was saying they had to work it our for themselves. But those guys are great musicians and they're great guys, and the truth is I don't want to go solo with a bunch of session musicians.**"** NOEL (2001)

"We were the first people to come out and say, 'The world's a great place, life is for living. Forget grunge music. Get a pint of Guinness down your neck, and pick that guitar up.'" NOEL (2005)

"We're touring till next March (2006), and I'd have thought by February we'll be sick of the sight of each other. We'll probably have the rest of the year out, and Liam will write 500 songs, Gem (Archer) and Andy (Bell) will write a few and I'll go back to the ones I haven't finished off.**"** NOEL (2005)

"We never make plans. We haven't got a record deal anyway. We're out of a deal, which is a great position to be in. So we're gonna have to find a new record deal that suits us, that's where we're at, and then we don't like to rush things." NOEL (2005)

"I'd like to go to Area 51 (rumoured American top-secret space research area) just to see what they are fucking doing there. If not, I'd like to go to the moon.**" NOEL (2003)**

"Maybe on cable we could get our own channel, just me and Liam telling it like it is." NOEL (2002)

"I'm 35 now and I think, there's nothing gonna happen to me in the next 35 years which hasn't happened already apart from dying.**"**

NOEL (2002)

THE FUTURE & NEW BEGINNINGS

❝I've been round the world 15 fucking times and I've seen every single thing there is to see. So it doesn't hold any great adventure to me. It's like doing a job which is why we get so bored.❞ NOEL (2003)

❝If he (Paul Weller) packs it in, I won't be far behind.**❞** NOEL (2002)

❝We're all heathens. Few of us practise a faith but we're after something. I'm after something. I'll say no more that that in case I start to sound like Thom Yorke.❞ NOEL (2002)

❝Part of us would love to release an album on the internet, just to frighten the living daylights out of the bastards (Sony BMG).**❞**

NOEL (2005)